The
NAME
IS
The
GAME

Onomatology and the Genealogist

Lloyd de Witt Bockstruck
alias **Niederbockstruck,** FNGS

CLEARFIELD

Published for Clearfield Company by
Genealogical Publishing Company
Baltimore, Maryland
2013

Library of Congress Catalog Card Number 2013930436

ISBN: 978-0-8063-5834-5

I would like to thank a number of colleagues who have shared their knowledge with me. They include John Frederick Dorman, FASG, of Fredericksburg, Virginia; Maxine Alcorn, formerly of the Clayton Library for Genealogical Research of the Houston Public Library; Brent Howard Holcomb of Columbia, South Carolina; Robert Scott Davis of Wallace State Community College, Hanceville, Alabama; David C. Dearborn, FASG, of the New England Historic Genealogical Society Library, Boston, Massachusetts; James Jeffreys of the Denver Public Library, Denver, Colorado; and Craig Scott of Holly Springs, North Carolina.

Table of Contents

The Name Is the Game: Onomatology and the Genealogist

Chapter 1 Introduction

I began the genealogical investigations of my family in 1963 because I was curious to learn from whence my forbears had come. Having six great-great-grandparents born in Europe, I rather quickly bridged the Atlantic Ocean to ancestral homes in the British Isles and on the Continent. Being a college student at the time, I made an appointment with the chairman of the Foreign Languages Department, Professor Wilson La Due, to ask him what the names of my five German great-great-grandparents meant. I was a bit surprised when he told me that one of them, Greenwood, was not a German surname at all. I knew my great-grandmother's brother, August Samuel Greenwood, quite well and often heard him speak in German. I also knew my great-grandmother's eldest daughter equally well and marveled as a child when she would converse with someone else in a language which was unintelligible to me. Her brother, my grandfather, was the first one in the family to learn English, but I could recall nothing more than his returning grace in German at mealtime or uttering expletives. Dr. LaDue explained that Greenwood was undoubtedly the English translation of the German word, Grunewald. I was not entirely satisfied with his explanation. It was the first time that I realized that the names of individuals were just like the vocabulary of any foreign language which had to be rendered into English. I located the marriage record of my great-grandparents in 1887, and my great-grandmother's maiden surname appeared as Greenwalt in that document. In a still earlier document she was living at home with her parents who were recorded in the 1860 census as Grunewald. With these three documents I had the evidence for Dr. LaDue's explanation even though I had had misgivings initially.

The Name Is the Game: Onomatology and the Genealogist

During my weekly visits with my paternal grandmother, who lived but two blocks from the college campus, I took time out from my academic studies and delighted in my interviews with her. On one occasion she and I spent an afternoon reviewing an entire box of photographs of friends and family members from yesteryear. While some of them were known unto me, many were not. One was a rather large group photograph of her relatives at her grandparents' family home, which her grandfather had built after emigrating from Rockenhausen, Rheinland Pfalz. My father and his younger brother were small children on the front row. I had already created family group sheets for the families of the siblings of my great-grandmother, and I now had their visual images as well. One elderly family member in the photograph was a woman very properly attired with a large brim hat, gloves, and handbag. I asked my grandmother who she was and learned that she was the sister of my grandmother's maternal grandfather. My grandmother had not mentioned her before, and I wondered why. She told me that the lady was Aunt Barbara Baker. Her husband died early in life, and their only son did not survive infancy. Even though the family photograph was undated, I calculated that it had to have been taken during World War I. I was ecstatic because it meant that Aunt Barbara Baker would surely have a death certificate with her mother's maiden name which I had been unable to learn. Her brother, my great-great-grandfather, Daniel Graff, died too early to have a death certificate, and his brothers, Michael Graff, Henry Graff, and Peter Graff, had certificates lacking their mother's maiden name. I knew there would be a fee for a search of the records in the county clerk's office, and I hoped that I could save some expense by being armed with the exact date of her death.

My grandmother's scrapbooks did not contain the obituary of Aunt Barbara; moreover, she had not begun her diaries until sometime after the death of Aunt Barbara. Even though my grandmother had astonished me by recalling the exact dates of death of dozens of other family members, she could not remember when Aunt Barbara died. My solution was to go to the cemetery to retrieve the date from her headstone. When I asked my grandmother where Aunt Barbara was buried, I learned it was in the town of St. Jacob, Illinois. I had never heard of any such place. She explained that it was in the adjoining county so I planned a visit on the next day I had free. When I arrived, I noted that the cemetery was a large one. I walked every row without finding the grave of Aunt Barbara Baker and repeated the search in the event that I had simply overlooked the marker. I had not. I returned home to tell my grandmother that if Aunt Barbara had been buried there, the large monument on her grave which my grandmother had described had been stolen. It was at that moment that my grandmother looked at my notes and saw how I had written the words "Barbara Baker." Any academic achievement I had attained disappeared from my grandmother's mind in an instant. She said that was not the way to spell Aunt Barbara's surname. It was Becker. I had simply overlooked the very headstone I was seeking because I had been searching for a grave with the wrong spelling. Of course, I was then a freshman in college and enrolled in French 101 rather than German 101 due to a scheduling conflict with a prerequisite class in my major. I did not realize that Becker was the German form of Baker. Both names are virtually identical when spoken in German. My rendering of Aunt Barbara's surname was an oral pitfall which could have plagued me even longer than it did.

It was necessary to return to the cemetery to learn the death date of Aunt Barbara Becker, and I found what I was seeking. Armed not only with the correct date of death, I also had the correct spelling for the name of the decedent in order to approach the county clerk in the proper county in my quest of her death certificate.

Predeceasing Aunt Barber Baker was a brother named Michael Graff. Once again I had erred because I recorded his name as Mitchell Graff which was the pronunciation my grandmother used. I had not been able to locate a death certificate for him because I did not recognize how to spell his forename.

The Name Is the Game: Onomatology and the Genealogist

Another lesson which I soon had to learn was that the spelling of the surname of Graff was not utilized by all of the members of the family. Indeed, my great-great-grandfather's Mexican War discharge certificate bore his name as Daniel Graf. He and at least three of his brothers adopted the spelling of Graff. His numerous first cousins in Miami and Howard Counties, Indiana held the first Graf family reunion in 1914 with more than one hundred and fifty in attendance, and none of them used the spelling of Graff. They used Graf. With such a slight spelling variation, I was never able to uncover why some members of the family added a second "f" to their surname.

Many years later as a librarian I was assisting a person engaged in researching her own ancestry. She told me that her grandmother was a Beecham from Tarrant County, Texas. I was unable to locate the grandmother in the 1880 census because I had assumed how to spell the surname and found no corresponding entry. When I shared my findings with the researcher, she looked at my notes and somewhat indignantly responded that the family's surname was spelled Beauchamp and not Beecham. Once again I had allowed myself to be misled by information gleaned orally and had not even considered a different written version.

Another example of meeting an ancestor only on paper involved Philip Moore who married Phebe Elam in Mecklenburg County, Virginia 21 December 1789. The annual tax lists of the county carried his name from the time of his attaining his majority until his removal to Rutherford County, North Carolina. In one year, however, he appeared as Philip Burroughs Moore. The clue of his middle name seemed promising. No one named Burroughs, however, appeared in any of the county's records or in those of any contiguous county. A thorough examination of the records did yield the clue leading to the correction needed to make any more progress. He appeared as Philip Burrus Moore in one record, and there were a number of generations of Philip Burruses in a family in nearby Surry County, Virginia. I was now able to resume the search and to extend his pedigree

The Name Is the Game: Onomatology and the Genealogist

because I knew that Burrus and Burroughs were the same surname.

I had learned that I needed to pay particular attention to the spelling of an ancestral surname with any variants in earlier records. Becoming acquainted with ancestors whom I had never met necessitated that I acquire the actual pronunciation rather than what I had assumed.

These examples are indicative of how important the study of naming practices is to the genealogist.

Onomatology is the study of names. It involves both forenames, commonly called first, second, or middle names, and family names or surnames. It also includes nicknames and place names which in the United States are often named for individuals.

In the heritage of the Western world, the earliest genealogical records mention individuals by their forenames since it was the church which generated the records. The church was concerned with the Christian names bestowed upon infants or converts. The church was not concerned with surnames and did not utilize them in its records for centuries. Even after surnames had come into widespread use, some contemporary indexes, (e.g. baptisms in parish registers) were created by forenames rather than by surnames.) Technically the church still recognizes the forename alone, as in baptism when the pastor or priest says "I baptize this child as Mary," and at marriage "Do you, John, take this woman, Mary, to be your lawful wedded wife?" Accordingly, the church–and by extension society in general– referred to forenames as Christian names. Preprinted legal forms used the same terminology well into the twentieth century in various states in the United States.

The Hebrew name Daniel, meaning "God has judged," was exclusively used for monks and bishops in the western world until the twelfth century. The name of the blessed Virgin, Mary, was long held to be

9

too sacred for common use. It first entered the British Isles in 1082 when King Malcolm and his wife Margaret of Scotland bestowed it upon their daughter. It did not enter Ireland until the seventeenth century where it eventually became the most common forename for females.

The ultimate question in genealogical research is "Who were the parents?" Genealogists sometimes tend to lose sight of the one ingredient common to every genealogical problem–the name of the individual. When they do, the consequences can be disastrous because ancestors do not exist in anonymity. Even when genealogists amass mountains of names, they sometimes seem unable to make any progress in extending their pedigree. It is no longer a question of what records exist that might not have been examined but rather one of considering the onomatological evidence in the records already searched and interpreting that evidence correctly.

William Shakespeare had his character, Juliet, ask "What's in a name?"; centuries later playwright Bertold Brecht seemed to be responding when he wrote that "A name is an uncertain thing; you can't count on it." Asking the right question is not the only element in a genealogical inquiry. Knowing how to reach the correct conclusion is even more important.

One of the most telling examples of onomatology as a tool for genealogical success involved a Scotsman named Ian Ferguson who came to the colony of New York. In time he made his way up the Hudson River from New York City to the juncture with the Mohawk River where he settled among the Palatine Germans whom Queen Anne had given safe haven. Since he was in the minority and most of the written records in the community were being made by the Palatines, he became known by the German equivalent of his name, Johann Feuerstein. In his latter years he removed to the colony of Pennsylvania where he settled in the second or third largest English speaking city in the world, Philadelphia, the city of Brotherly Love. There he appeared in the records as John Flint because his name had been rendered into English. Two generations later following the

The Name Is the Game: Onomatology and the Genealogist

Louisiana Purchase, one of his grandsons, Peter Flint, left the City of Brotherly Love and joined the westward movement to make his fortune. He located in Louisiana near the mouth of the Mississippi River which was the commercial center of Trans-Appalachia. There the prevailing language was French so he was absorbed into the culture and appeared in records as Pierre a Fusil. Prior to the Civil War he moved back to civilization, i.e. Texas, and the French form of his surname became Gunn in English. Somewhat ironically the original surname, Ferguson, is Scottish as is Gunn. Howard F. Barker wrote "What changes names most is the abrasion of common speech," and his observation captures the essence of onomatology and genealogy.

The study of onomatology is one based on records over centuries and requires an awareness of a multitude of changes in names; however here are a few basics.

Surnames first appeared among the families of southern Europe, particularly in Spain and Italy where families derived their surnames from their landed estates and castles in the tenth century. Their landed estates descended in the male line so it was logical that surnames did as well. By the twelfth century surnames had spread across the Alps into Switzerland and down the Rhine Valley. By the 14th century surnames were common in Germany and in the British Isles. By the 19th century surnames were in use across the European continent. Wales and the Shetland Islands were the last parts of the United Kingdom where people adopted surnames. Surnames worked their way down the social ladder from the nobility to the aristocracy, the bourgeois, and lastly the peasants. Commerce was the major factor prompting the adoption of surnames among urban dwellers.

Surnames in Iceland are quiet recent. A child has a patronymic using the father's given name in the genitive with the Icelandic suffix of "son" or "dottir." For that reason lists of Icelanders, such as telephone directories, are arranged alphabetically by forename.

The Name Is the Game: Onomatology and the Genealogist

In France Francois I in 1539 made it mandatory that forenames had to be approved by a priest and officially registered. In Christendom the clergy in other countries also insisted upon the use of Christian forenames although classical names were the first to erode the practice.

The English practice in the use of surnames does not necessarily transfer to other nationalities. Spanish, French, New Netherland Dutch, and Italian women in America retained their maiden names after marriage even though their children inherited the surname of their father. This ancestral practice, however, eventually yielded to the Anglo pattern. The same is true in Scotland where a woman will appear under her maiden name as the wife of her husband on their gravestone. In Goochland County, Virginia is a marriage bond issued to Samuel Pryor to marry Frances Meriwether, widow of Nicholas Meriwether, on 27 August 1760. On the same day the Rev. William Douglas married the couple and recorded in his register that he celebrated the marriage and reported the names of the groom and bride as Samuel Pryor and ffrances Morton, so even in English speaking families a married female can be known by her maiden name to which she reverted after her marriage in her widowhood.

The letters "X" and "p" represents the Greek letters X (Ch) and p (r) for Christ and are incorporated into both surnames and forenames in written records. It persists in the abbreviation Xmas for the holiday of Christmas. Christopher would be written as Xopher. Christian would be written as Xian. Both could also have been abbreviated in English as Christ. The capital letter "F" was often written as a pair of lower case "ff's as in ffleet and ffrancis. The thorn closely resembles the letter "y" and represents the sound of "th" so "yat" and "yem" are actually that and them. Yomas would be Thomas. It is not to be confused with the pronoun "ye" which is the singular form of the second person in English. Ye Old Curiosity Shop would be pronounced as The Old Curiosity Shop because the first word is an adjective, and not the pronoun ye for the singular of you, and begins with the letter form thorn.

The Name Is the Game: Onomatology and the Genealogist

Theophilus Taylor was a settler in the Carolina piedmont. At the time of his arrival in the British colonies he bore the name of Gotlieb Schneider. He eventually translated both his forename and surname into English and became Theophilus Taylor. Making that discovering ought to have allowed a genealogical researcher to bridge the Atlantic Ocean and to locate his baptismal entry in his village of origin in Germany. The entry in parish register, however, was actually in Latin, and his name appeared as Amadeus Sartor. The lack of such knowledge could cause the relevant entry in the record to be overlooked. Such an example is typical of the onomatological challenges confronting the genealogist. Knowing the foreign language equivalent of someone in America with his or her language of origin may also require a knowledge of rendering a name in Latin.

Another example of multi-language renderings involves John Wood who had previously been known as Johann Wald in his native Germany but was baptized as Jean DuBois in the German speaking portion of western France.

Patrick Hanks' *Dictionary of American Family Names* (New York, N.Y.: Oxford University Press, 2003)is a three-volume set which is the most encyclopedic source in coverage and reflects the most current scholarship in onomatology. It is the first source to consult in order to ascertain the language(s) of origin of any surname.

Some surnames in the United States can be isolated to a specific location within one of the colonies. Eibach is a Swiss surname localized in the area of Craven County, North Carolina. It has proliferated into a host of spellings including Apock, Ebach, Epagh, Hubbach, Hypock, Ibach, Impock, Ipach, Ipock, Ispach, Ispack, Slobbach, Slopak, Spock, and Ybach, Any surname which begins with a vowel [a, e, i, o, u, w, h, and y] may be manifested in such variations.

13

The Name Is the Game: Onomatology and the Genealogist

The Name Is the Game: Onomatology and the Genealogist

Chapter 2 Forenames

In his poem, "Just 'fore Christmas," Eugene Field wrote:

> Father calls me William,
> Sister calls me Will,
> Mother calls me Willie,
> But the fellers call me Bill.

While most American researchers would recognize all of these four as the same party, other instances are not so likely to be so.

Ethnic Clues in Forenames

The forenames of Duncan, Colin, Neil, Kenneth, Gavin, Nicol, Flora, Hugh, Alexander, Agnes, Jean, Janet, and Isabella are Scottish in origin. Douglas, Donald, Kenneth, Ian, Neil, and Stewart were favored by the Highlanders from Scotland. Patrick, Terence, and Dennis are Irish, but Patrick was popular for all of Ireland including the Protestants in Ulster Plantation. Felix, Christian, Ulrich, Benedict, and Vincent are from the German-speaking part of Switzerland. Wendell, Sebastian, Sigismund, and Cunigunde are German. Teunis is Dutch. Evan, Owen, and Rhys are Welsh. Recognizing the language of the forename may very well be an asset in laying out one's research strategy—particularly when the bearer has translated his or her surname.

Forename or a Title

The surnames of Ensign, Sargent, Corporal, and Major are often bestowed on sons of a man's daughters as forenames and should not be confused with military rank. Thomas and Hannah Mann named their son, Ensign Mann, in Scituate, Massachusetts. Judge is another surname used as a forename and is not indicative of a judicial officer. While squire designated a local judge, it can also be a forename as in the example of Squire Boone. There was a General Jackson McCoy whose name was changed to General Jackson Cameron in 1857 in Missouri. General was a forename and not his military title. It is necessary to examine a number of records to determine which interpretation is correct for such an individual.

The Maiden Name of a Mother as a Forename
The earliest recorded case dates from the sixteenth century. It involved the English lord, Guilford Dudley, whose mother's maiden name was Guilford. Other examples include Ashley, Beverley, Cecil, Douglas, Duncan, Howard, Keith, Lloyd, Sidney, Stuart, Stanley, and Tiffany.

It was said of Judge Andrew McConnel January Cochran of the Federal District Court of Kentucky that he was "an aristocratic scion of a whole string of pioneer families, several of which were represented in his name."

Forename Clues
In New England many descendants of Thomas Prince through maternal lines bear his surname as their forename. In the south, however, Prince was a forename which was used by African Americans for their sons.

The use of surnames as forenames was a means by which families could show their connections and strengthen the solidarity of the elite. Humbler families also adopted the practice. The practice tended to favor sons over daughters. Robert Beheathland of Jamestowne, Virginia arrived in 1607 and became the first American head of a family to have no male heirs to perpetuate the surname. He was survived by his two daughters. With his death the line had "daughtered" out. The descendants of his daughter, Mary, used Beheathland for females in their branch of the family, and the descendants of his other daughter, Dorothy, used Beheathland for males.

Regional differences also governed the choice of forenames. In Puritan New England nearly ninety per cent of the forenames were biblical in origin. Elsewhere less than half of the forenames were biblical. While the Puritans disdained the use of the names of the archangels, Gabriel and Michael, families in the South did not. The forename of Paul was also rather rare among the Puritans because of its association with Roman Catholicism. The forename of Luther for a Roman Catholic would probably be an ancestral surname and not for the Protestant Reformer, Martin Luther.

Among Germans the forenames of Franz and Xavier were predominately used by Roman Catholics and may narrow the geographical search process or eliminate the need of reading Protestant parish registers in the quest of a child's baptismal record in a locality with both branches of Christianity. Reigning German monarchs also account for the popularity of their forenames among their subjects. The ducal forenames of Eberhard, Ludwig, and Ulrich might well suggest an origin in Wurttemberg while Bernard, Phillip, and Frederick could be indicative of a Badenese origin.

The forename of Benoni is Hebrew for "child of my sorrow." In the Old Testament he was the child of Jacob and Rachel. His mother died after his birth, and his father changed his name to Benjamin. Accordingly, Benoni became a forename for a male whose mother died in or shortly following childbirth. Of course, many sons and grandsons of men named Benoni were given the forename of Benoni in honor of their father or grandfather. They did not have a mother who died given them birth, so one cannot always rely on the supposition that the mother of someone named Benoni was to one who had lost his mother in or following his birth.

If the father of an unborn child died before the birth of his child and

17

the child was a son, the child might be named Ichabod. In the Old Testament Phineas and his father Eli died. When the wife of Phineas learned of their deaths, she went into labor and delivered a son whom she named Ichabod. It is a good clue that a babe's father did not live to see the male child his wife was carrying. Ichabod was a common Biblical forename in New England and New York but not in the South.

The forename of Hiram is distinctive to the United States where its popularity was due to the growth of the fraternal organization of Freemasonry in which Hiram is a major character in that society.

Certain forenames can point to a geographical origin. The forename of Levin in the seventeenth and eighteenth century points to an origin in the colony of Maryland or the Delmarva Peninsula. The forename of Ignatius in English families also points to Maryland where Roman Catholics were some of the original colonists. Other ethnic groups, such as the Palatines, also used the forename regardless in which colony they might have settled. Sabra and Kerrenhappuck, especially the latter, are more common in Virginia than in New England. Drury is a male forename common in Southside Virginia where it is found as early as 1685. David was rare in New England and the Delaware River Valley but common in the South. Quakers and Puritans did not admire his Biblical antics as being one to be emulated. The female forenames of Persis and Calista were in vogue in colonial New England but not in the other colonies. One of the earliest known instances of the use of the forename of Calista occurred in Brimfield, Massachusetts when John and Ruth Danielson named their daughter, Calista Danielson. She was born 28 February 1758. The forename became popular in the area of Worcester County and in Connecticut. By the 1820s it was extremely popular and appeared in westward migrating families from the two most populous New England states of Massachusetts and Connecticut.

The female names of Emblem, Concurrence, and Olive were quite popular in Woodberry, Connecticut and tended to be peculiar to that New England town.

Theodorick was a forename almost exclusively found among colonial Virginians.

Grace names were widespread in New England but were also found in the Middle Colonies. Richard and Abigail Lippincott's eight children were named Remember born 15 Mar. 16– Dorchester, Mass. [,] John born 7 Oct. 16– Boston, Mass. [,] Restore born Plymouth 3 July 165- [,] Freedom born Stonehouse, England 1 Aug. 165-[,] Increase born Stonehouse, England 5 Dec. 1657 [,] Jacob born Stonehouse, England 11 May 1660 [,] Preserve born 25 Mar. 1663 in Rhode Island [, and] Israel. All of the children were males except Increase. The children's forenames almost constituted a prayer. The family became Quakers and settled in Shrewsbury, New Jersey.

Isham, pronounced Isom, was a surname found in Southside Virginia where Henry Isham left no issue. His heirs were his sisters who perpetuated their connection by using Isham as a forename for their issue. Tryphosia and Tryphena are much more prevalent female forenames in New England than in the southern colonies.

There are also denominational religious affiliations reflected in the choice of forenames. The wife of William Penn was named Gulielma so that her forename became widespread among Quaker families. Methodist families bestowed the names of such divines as John Wesley, Francis Asbury, and Lorenzo Dow on their sons. Among the Amish the forenames of Menno, Amos, Jonas, Levi, Mahlon, and Phineas were common. If a colonial American family with a common German surname, e.g. Mueller, exists with members bearing these forenames, that would be a particularly helpful clue in formulating a research strategy by eliminating Lutherans, Reformed, and Roman Catholics families with the same surname.

The Name Is the Game: Onomatology and the Genealogist

In the Jordan family of Virginia the forename of River was popular for male children. The same sense of humor manifested itself in New England with the forename of Preserved in the Fish Family. In Lancaster County, South Carolina in the 1800 census was Night Knight.

Americans descended from nineteenth and twentieth century immigrants need to be aware that forenames of other European languages might not correspondent to the presumed English equivalent. The Italian forename of Vincenzo might be expected to be rendered as Vincent but in practice would be James. Rosario would be Ronald, and Santo would be Samuel.

Diminutives

A diminutive is the familiar form of a forename used by family members and close friends. Originally it arose when parents gave the same forename to two different children. Today male diminutives are much more likely to be recognized than are their female counterparts. Bob was the diminutive for Robert, Jim for James, Joe for Joseph, Bill for William, Jerry for Jeremiah, Harry for Henry, and Johnny for John. Leo arose as a diminutive for Leonidas or Leopold. Mollie, Molly, and Polly were diminutives of Mary. Sally was the diminutive of Sarah. Patsey, Patty, and Mat were diminutives of Martha. Peggy was the diminutive of Margaret. Meg also came into wide use as the diminutive of Margaret with the publication of Louisa Mae Alcott's *Little Women.* Lena was the diminutive for Elenora, Helena, and Magdalena. Rine was the diminutive of Catherine. Mabel was the diminutive of Mehitabel, and Dolly for Dorothy. (Dorothy was also the feminine diminutive of Theodora.) Tenty was a diminutive of Content. Ricka or Rickey was the diminutive of both Frederica and Ulrica. Jennie was more commonly the diminutive for Jane, but it was also a diminutive for Virginia and Genevieve. Ed could have been the diminutive for Edgar, Edward, Edwin, or Edmund. Van was the diminutive of Sylvanus. Dutch families in America, such as the Van Sweargins, may sever the prefix from the surname and use it as a forename instead. Sandy and

Zandy were diminutives of Alexander. Oph, sometimes spelled phonetically as Off, was the diminutive of Theophilus, and Cassie was for Cassandra. Seba was the female diminutive of Sybil. Lista was the diminutive of Calista. Amy was the diminutive of both Naomi and Amelia. While Cass was a surname, it was also a diminutive of Caswell and of Cassius.

Illustrative of the difficulty of diminutives involved Col. Henry Dixon of North Carolina. His heirs sought his commutation of five years' full pay in the Revolutionary War. They did not establish their case by testimony and did not prove that he died in the service. The heirs were able to demonstrate in April 1793 that $360 had been paid to him or to his heirs. Regardless. Congress in 1835 ruled that he was not eligible for commutation. The payment could have been a pension, but his name did not appear on the list of pensioners. The heirs or their legal representative had failed to recognize that one Harry Dixon was a lieutenant colonel from North Carolina and that he died in the service on 17 July 1782. His widow, Martha Dixon, and seven children applied for a pension from Caswell County in 1786. The failure to recognize that Harry was the diminutive of Henry denied the family the benefits which they so rightly deserved.

The forename of Rees can be the diminutive of Reason. It can also be a variant spelling of the Welsh forename of Rhys. The surname of Duke may appear to become a forename, but it may be the diminutive of Marmaduke.

Bias was the diminutive of Tobias as was Toby. The book of Tobias is found in the Roman Catholic and Orthodox Bibles but not in most Protestant Bibles so its appearance in a family could be indicative of religious preference.

Some diminutives would not always be recognized as such but interpreted to be distinct forenames. Luke and Luther are such an example as are Peter and Patrick.

The Name Is the Game: Onomatology and the Genealogist

Fate and Lafe were diminutives of Lafayette and appeared in the Revolutionary War for sons named in honor of the Marquis de Lafayette, who had come to America to aid in the struggle for Independence. Lum was for Columbus, and Kit for Christopher. Topher and Tofer were diminutives for Christopher. Hetty was normally the diminutive of Harriet. In the South, however, it could also represent the forename of Beheathland.

Doctor was often used as a nickname for the seventh son in a family because it was believed that a seventh son had an intuitive knowledge of the use of herbs. It could, however, be a forename as it was for Doctor Willard Bliss who ironically actually became a physician. As Dr. Doctor Willard Bliss, he attended President James A. Garfield as he was dying.

Diminutives of German forenames found in America include Stoffel for Christopher, Bascht for Sebastian, Felty for Valentine, Poldi for Leopold, Fritz for Frederick, Rudy for Rudolph or Reudiger, Heinz for Heinrich, and Gretha for Margaretha. Sometimes the suffix "-schen" meaning little was added to the forename, as in the example of Hanschen for little John and Gretchen for little Margaret. The suffix "-lein" is another way of creating a German diminutive so that Hanslein is the diminutive of Johannes. It is important to remember that in such examples the final two letters were not the feminine form of a German surname. The suffix diminutive, "-el" meaning little, was also German as in Hansel and Gretel.

In New Netherland, Thys was the diminutive for Matthys, Claes for Nicolass, Nys for Denys, Cobus for Jacobus, and Jaap for Jacob. Krelis was the diminutive of Cornelis. Bartel, Mees, and Meus were diminutives of Barthelmeus.

Nicknames Past and Present: A List of Nicknames for Given Names in the Past and Present Time (San Jose, Calif.: C. R. Publications, 2007) by Christine Rose, F.A.S.G., is the most inclusive and authoritative work available for the American genealogist on the subject.

The Name Is the Game: Onomatology and the Genealogist

Diminutive Abbreviations

It is important to be aware of such situations so that one does not overlook relevant entries in the records. Jos. could represent Josiah, Joseph, Joshua, Josephat, or Josephus. Abe could represent Abraham, Absalom, Abel, Abijah, or Abimilech. Eli could be Eli in its own right as well as the familiar form of Eliphalet, Eliphas, or Elihu. Mar. could be Maria, Mary, Margaret, Mariah, or Martha. Nathan could be a forename in its own right, or it could be the diminutive of Nathaniel. Richd. most commonly represented Richard, but it could also be for Richmond. Theo. could be the abbreviation of Theobald, Theophilus, Theodorick, Theodore, or Theodosius. Sy could be Cyrus, Josiah, or Cyril. Lon was the diminutive of Alonzo and Leonidas. Amy was the diminutive of Naomi. While Lot might seem to be a variant spelling of Lott, it was actually the diminutive of Lancelot. Neil was the diminutive of Cornelius, and Robin was a diminutive of Robert. Andrew had as its diminutives Drew and Andy. Hepsibah had Hepsey for its diminutive as well as the unaspirated version, Epsey. Lois was a colonial counterpart of Louisa, and Cump was for Tecumseh as in William Tecumseh Sherman, the Civil War General. Will could represent William, Willard, Wilbur, or Wilford, Alfy could be the diminutive of Alfred, Alpheus, or Alfonzo. Kirk was the diminutive of the male forename, Lycurgus. Ben could represent Benjamin, but it might also be the diminutive of Benedict or Benoni.

Dusty is an example of a forename distinctive to a specific family–the Rhodes.

It is not always apparent that a forename is a diminutive. The forename of Hugh is one such example. It may also be the diminutive of Elihu whereby the suffix of the forename becomes the familiar form of address.

In courthouses which use the Campbell index to provide access to their land and probate records, it can be especially difficult to locate the relevant record(s) if an individual is indexed under his or her diminutive unless a researcher knows of all the possibilities. Since such records were created by clerks and deputy clerks over centuries, one is likely to find entries for the same person under his or her forename and under his or her diminutive. The Campbell index is arranged by the initial letter of the surname and the initial letter of the forename and widely scatters individuals of the same surname recorded under both their diminutives and full-forms of their forenames.

Forename Equivalents

The English name of Jane has as its Scottish counterpart Jean, and more than one researcher has concluded that a man had a first wife named Jean and a second wife named Jane when in fact there was only one spouse. Another Scottish female forename, Agnes, was Nancy in English. Daniel and Donald were the equivalents of each other in Scotland. Hamish was Gaelic for James, and Ian for John. Other interchangeable names include Isobel and Elizabeth. Ann could have been Agnes or Annis. Hester and Esther were inter-changeable as were Helen and Ellen. Augustine may also appear as Austin which was the oral equivalent. Mercy in colonial New England was pronounced as Marcy, which spelling was frequently used.

If a record is in Latin, some forenames are not readily identified by their English counterpart. Hieronymus, for example, is the Latin for Jerome and Abdias is for Obediah. The German male forename, Emil, derived from the Latin Augustus. While Eugenius was recognizable as Eugene, it may also have represented Owen. Dionisius was the Latin counterpart of Dennis; its feminine form was Dionesia for Denise. Appolonia was identical in English and Latin, but it may also have represented Pauline. Margareta may have represented Margaret or Pearl. Aloysius was the Latin version of Lewis, and Milo for Miles.

A very helpful work giving versions of forenames on a language

24

The Name Is the Game: Onomatology and the Genealogist

basis is *Foreign Versions of English Names and Foreign Equivalents of United States Military and Civilian Titles* (Detroit, Mich.: Grand River Books,
(197-).

Multiple Forenames

Since it was the church which regulated forenames, the church's view was that a person could have only one baptismal name. One of the earliest breaks with tradition in America involved the family of Henry Winthrop who married Elizabeth Fones. They named their daughter, Martha Johanna Winthrop, when she was born 9 May 1630. In the seventeenth century in America parents bestowed the entire name of a forbear upon their child. Abner and Mary Grigg of Bristol Parish, Virginia named their daughter Mary Ford Grigg incorporating the full maiden name of the child's mother. In New England Daniel and Hannah (Swift) Wing named a son Samuel Batchelder Wing when he was born 28 August 1652.

In Europe, especially in the German speaking areas, it became fashionable for a child to be given a string of forenames the last of which was the one by which the parents intended for the infant to be known. It was called a Rufname. It was not necessarily binding for life. The adult bearer could chose any of his or her forenames as the one by which he or she wished to be known.

Uxornecronyms

Families with a husband having two wives in succession involves the challenge of attributing the children to the correct mother. Aaron Smith married firstly Sarah Gately, daughter of Jemima Gately, in 1812 in Caldwell County, Kentucky. She died as a young woman. Twelve years later he married secondly Mary Laughlin. In his will he named a daughter Sally Gately Smith. Determining which wife was her mother was the important genealogical question.

The Name Is the Game: Onomatology and the Genealogist

An uxornecronym is the name of the first daughter born unto a second wife honoring the name of the first wife, who had died, so Mary Laughlin was the mother of Sally Gately Smith. Ignorance of this practice could lead to the wrong interpretation of the data.

In New Netherland Jan Pieterszen Van Huysen named the first daughter by his second wife, Grietje, Jans Elsje. The Dutch traditionally named the second daughter after a grandmother, but neither Jan nor Grietje had a mother named Elsje. That forename was the one borne by his first wife.

Ambisexual Forenames

In the English-speaking world some forenames are ambisexual, i.e. they are bestowed upon both males and females. Marion is probably the most common. The quality names, e.g. Obedience and Remember, are borne by both genders. Some of ambisexual forenames are seldom recognized as in the case of Florence. They may have slightly different spellings. Jesse, for example, has as its female counterpart Jessie. Francis has its female counterpart Frances. In pre-twentieth century records, however, the spelling cannot be relied upon to designate the correct gender.

Among Roman Catholics whose language is German or Spanish, Maria is used for both genders. Erich Maria Remarque, author of *All Quiet on the Western Front,* and Jose Maria Martinez are examples of males bearing a female forename. When the forename Maria comes first, as in Maria Jose Lopez, the person is a female. When it is preceded by a male forename, the child is indeed a male. The French also used Marie for males, but like the Spanish and Germans, it followed a male forename or was hyphenated as Jean-Marie Dube. There are also Englishmen who bear the name of Maria. One of the most notable was Edward Maria Wingfield, a founder of the colony of Virginia. He was the son of Thomas Maria Wingfield, who was the godson of Maria, Queen of England.

The Name Is the Game: Onomatology and the Genealogist

Henry and Bennett are female diminutives of Henrietta and Benedicta so that civil marriage records involving brides with these diminutives might be misconstrued as a marriage between two males rather than a groom and a bride. The masculine forename of Michael has as its counterpart the feminine Michal. The latter enjoyed widespread popularity in the South and reveals the significance of the spelling as to the gender of the bearer.

Postponing the Bestowing of Forenames

The high incidence of child mortality caused parents to wait enough time to learn if the baby was going to survive before having the infant named. There are numerous examples of children as old as three years in the federal decennial census records enumerated with no forename but merely as Baby, as in the example of John and Sophia Crelsenburgh with their three-year old child in Steuben County, New York in 1860. They were taking as much precaution as possible to insure that the babe would survive infancy and childhood before giving the child a forename. The delay also reassured the parents that they would not have to repeat a forename in the event of the death of an infant or babe.

Repetition of Forenames

In New England families who had the sad misfortune to lose a child to
death would name the next child of the same gender with the same forename. They were determined to have a child to continue the identity. Necronyms appeared as often as eight per cent of the time in New England, but in the South Anglicans tended to avoid necronyms out of fear of bad luck. In Bristol Parish, Virginia, however, Drury and Amy Oliver named their daughter Martha at birth on 25 November 1724. The child died 27 September 1726, and they named their next child Martha born on 27 May 1727, so the principle was also practiced among Anglicans in the South.

The appearance of two children in the same family with the same forename does not necessarily imply that the first one died young. The practice arose in England to preserve intact a lease for three lives. Such a document required that the names of the parties be given.

One of the most powerful reasons for choosing a forename of a child were the names of the godparents, and this accounts for more than one child with the same forename in a family.

Edmund and Agnes (Austin) Littlefield of Wells, Maine, had two sons named Francis. In his will of 11 December 1661, Edmund Littlefield referred to sons Francis Littlefield, Sr. and Francis Littlefield, Jr. Both sons were the offspring of his wife, Agnes Littlefield, and both were alive.

In Henrico County, Virginia William and Elizabeth (?Littleberry) Worsham were the parents of a daughter Mary Worsham who married Richard Ligon. After William Worsham died, his widow married Col. Francis Epes, himself a widower. Elizabeth Epes also survived her second husband. She made her will 28 August 1678, and named as a legatee her daughter Mary Worsham. On the 23 September 1678, she made a second will and named her daughter Mary Epes as a legatee. The correct interpretation of the evidence is that Elizabeth (?Littleberry) Worsham Epes had two daughters named Mary–one by each of her husbands. The daughters were half-sisters. An inexperienced genealogist might have construed from the evidence that her daughter Mary Worsham had married between 28 August and 23 September and became Mary Epes merging two parties into one.

William Saeyn or Seyns, a colonial German, whose surname was Anglicized to Sign, named his daughters Catherine and Catherine, Jr. in his will of 24 April 1789, in Shenandoah County, Virginia. John Adam Kelp and John Adam Kelp, Jr. were named as sons of John Peter Kelp in a survey for land in the Northern Neck of Virginia when their brother, William Kelp, transferred the land to them on 3 January 1754.

The Name Is the Game: Onomatology and the Genealogist

John Lay of Lyme, Connecticut made his will 16 January 1674/5, and named his son John Lay whom he had by his former wife. He also named his sons Peter Lay and John Lay whom he had by his present wife. Another son was named James Lay. When James Lay died, he named in his will in 1682 his elder brother, John Lay, Sr., and his younger brother, John Lay, Jr.

Sarah Waterman of Norwich, Connecticut married firstly Thomas Sluman. One of their five children was named Sarah Sluman. Sarah (Waterman) Sluman married secondly Capt. John Wattles of Lebanon, Connecticut, a widower, with children one of whom was named Sarah Wattles. John and Sarah (Waterman) (Sluman) Wattles also had a daughter whom they named Sarah. The latter, therefore, had a maternal half-sister named Sarah and a paternal half-sister also named Sarah.

Ensign George Clark of Milford, Connecticut was married three times. By his first wife he had a daughter named Abigail born 1 April 1680, who married Joseph Talcott and died 24 March 1704. By his third wife he also had a daughter named Abigail in honor of her older half-sister who died before she was born. In his will, George Clark named the two sons of his daughter, Abigail Talcott, deceased. He also named his daughter, Abigail Curtis, the wife of Ebenezer Curtis.

Senior and Junior did not necessarily imply that the younger was the child of the elder of the same forename. The terms applied to both males and females. Two people in the same community could have no genealogical connection whatsoever even though they had the same name, so the terms do not imply any blood kinship. If there were more than two Sabra Elams as members of Liberty Baptist Church, the practice was to designate the eldest senior, the next junior, the next the 3rd, and the youngest the 4th. If the one bearing the designation junior moved out of the community, the 3rd would become junior, and the 4th would become the 3rd. The terms applied strictly to the living in a given community and were adjusted to reflect the situation at any given time. James Foster, 5th stated that he was the son of James Foster, 3rd when he had his name changed to Josiah Lovett Foster in 1829. In no case does the designation senior or junior following a party's forename and surname become part of one's legal identity.

John Hays of Augusta County, Virginia made his will on Christmas Day 1750, and it was proved 26 February 1750/1. He named his wife Rebecca Hays; his sons Andrew Hays, Charles Hays, and John Hays; his nephew John Hays, Jr.; his nephew Rebecca Hays the daughter of John Hays; his daughter Jenett Mills; his nephew Rebecky Guines; his nephew Robert Lusk; his nephew James Hays, the son of his son James Hays; and Abigail Hayes alias Kinseys. He was apparently anticipating his imminent death and did not style himself senior but instead accorded that designation by implication to his son of the same forename and called his grandson John Hays, Jr. His use of the term nephew designated a grandchild.

If a husband happened to have married women of the same forename, he may have had a child by each of his wives with the same forename. John Tarpley of Richmond County, Virginia had two wives named Elizabeth and each wife had a son named John. Hannah Lee of the Lees of Stratford Hall had a daughter Martha by her husband Gowin Corbin and another daughter named Martha by her second husband Richard Hall.

The use of numbers was always based on the Hindu-Arabic nomenclature in the English speaking world. Reigning monarchs, the pope, and members of the Reuss family in Germany were the only parties known by Roman numerals. In the Reuss family every male bore the name of Henry in honor of the Holy Roman Emperor Henry VI, who bestowed the territories of Weida and Gera upon the family. In the nineteenth century John Jacob Astor was the first American family to adopt the practice of using Roman numerals. Because the Astors did so, New York City's other socially prominent families, such as the Vanderbilts and Rockefellers, followed suit. Today Americans from all classes of society appear with

The Name Is the Game: Onomatology and the Genealogist

Roman numerals although the rest of the English speaking world does not follow this somewhat embarrassing practice.

Henry Kendall and Mary Jane (Speed) Briggs named their first daughter Clara Briggs. She was born 1 September 1855 and died early in life. Their second child was also a daughter and was named Clara Fillmore Briggs born 5 January 1857. Their third child was Emma J. Briggs born 22 January 1858. She too died young. Their fourth child was a son named Edward Wells Briggs born 8 February 1860. Their fifth child was a daughter named Nellie E. Briggs born 9 October 1869. She died 1 September 1870. They named their last daughter Nellie Gertrude Briggs when she was born 9 January 1872. Accordingly, they repeated the forenames of two sets of daughters because the first died young, and they wanted the forenames to survive.

Among the Germans the Christian names of John and Mary were two of the most important saints in Christendom. German families might give every son in the family the first forename of Johann and every daughter the first forename of Maria. They would always have a second or even a third or fourth forename one of which was the name by which the child would be known. Accordingly, a family of brothers named Johann Heinrich, Johann Friedrich, Johann Casper, Johann Ludwig, and Johann Wilhelm would have been known by their second forenames. If a German family wanted a son to be known as John, they would have had him baptized Johannes. He would have had no other forename as in the example of the composers, Johannes Brahms, as opposed to Johann Sebastian Bach.

Forename Clues

The Germans of colonial New York and New Jersey had a practice which can be very useful in identifying parents. For example, Leonard Ulmer had a son who was baptized as Johann Adam Ulmer. When the son attained his majority, he added his father's forename as his middle initial to his name so that Johann Adam Ulmer became Adam L. Ulmer. The custom

The Name Is the Game: Onomatology and the Genealogist

is a very useful tool for anticipating the forename of a boy's father and to avoid overlooking a relevant baptismal entry.

Hagiographic Forenames

Among Roman Catholic and Orthodox families children received their forenames from the saint's day on which they were born or the day of their baptism. It was the Council of Trent of 1566 that required that Roman Catholic babes be given the name of a saint. In Spanish-speaking countries the sixth of January is Dia de los Reyes, or the Day of the Wise Men. Children born on this day might be baptized Melchor Gasper Baltaser for the traditional three Magi , or Maria Reyes for the Mary the Mother of God. If the birth date of a person is not known, the date and month can be determined by learning the date of the saint's day which the child bore as his or her forename. It can expedite the search of unindexed baptismal entries in a parish register. There is also the possibility, however, that a child was given the name of a grandparent who was named for a saint's day.

Martin Luther limited saintly forenames to those mentioned in the scriptures so that non-scriptural forenames would be indicative of Roman Catholic Germans.

Naming Patterns

There is a widespread belief that specific naming patterns were in vogue in America before the twentieth century. While the locality and the ethnicity of families can influence the choice of forenames, the existence of naming patterns is rather rare.

There were two countries which have had highly developed systems of naming children. One was Scotland where the eldest son was named for the paternal grandfather, the second son after the maternal grandfather, the third son after the father, the eldest daughter for the maternal grandmother, the second daughter for the paternal grandmother, and the third daughter after the mother. Other children would be named after other members of the

The Name Is the Game: Onomatology and the Genealogist

family at the parents' discretion.

This pattern, however, can be rather easily upset. For example, Alexander McLain would have named his third son for himself, Alexander McLain, Jr. The third son. Alexander McLain, Jr., would have given his first born son the name of Alexander McLain in honor of the child's paternal grandfather. Therefore, Alexander McLain, Jr. could not have another son to be named for himself since he already had a son of that forename. The pattern was also disrupted when both grandfathers or both grandmothers had the same forename. If the maternal grandfather was a man of more prominence in the community, the eldest son might be named in his honor rather than for the paternal grandfather. It was also the custom to name a child for a recently installed minister in the parish rather than for a family member. Another deviation from the pattern occurred when the babe was the first one delivered by a doctor and received the forename of the doctor rather than that of an ancestor.

The other country with a naming pattern was that of the Netherlands. The Dutch in New Netherland and others who joined them, e.g. the Huguenots and Walloons, followed the same pattern. The eldest son bore the forename of the paternal grandfather, and the second son the name of the maternal grandfather. The first and second daughters honored the maternal and paternal grandmothers respectively. If a grandparent had more money or a higher social position, that grandparent would take precedence in the naming pattern. If a child had died, the Dutch gave the forename to the next child of that gender sometimes displacing a grandparent from the naming sequence pattern. If a grandparent were already dead, he or she was to be honored with the first child of the same gender.

Elbert Elbettse Stoothoff named his first son Gerret Elberts Stoothoff in honor of his wife's previous husband, Gerrit Wolpherts van Couwenhoven, so the pattern is not a rigid one.

The Name Is the Game: Onomatology and the Genealogist

There is a tradition among Italian families to name the first son and the first daughter after their paternal grandfather and paternal grandmother. The second son and second daughter received the forenames of their maternal grandfather and maternal grandmother. If a family member had recently died, the pattern might not have been observed. The family member who was the intended one to have a child named in his or her honor might have foregone the recognition in memory of the deceased.

Optical Mis-recognition
The Civil War service record for Edison Swimpfield is a difficult one to locate because it was mis-read when the records were indexed. His name was interpreted as Eitson Surmpfield. He served in Company F of the 16th Battalion of the Neal's Tennessee Cavalry. Manipulating the on-line index and reading the microfilm would not likely enable someone to locate his military record. Scanning the published index offers the best technique to locate an individual whose name had been incorrectly rendered in part due to the number of characters in his name.

Forenames from Historical Figures
One of the earliest examples in America was the birth of a son to John and Hannah (Smith) Laboyteaux on 17 September 1775. He was named George Washington Laboyteaux in honor of the commanding Revolutionary War General, His Excellency George Washington. The babe was the first of untold thousands of Americans who were named in honor of the first President. People recorded under initials such as G. W., T. J., J. Q. A., J.D., J. M., A. J., O. H. P., and J. K. P., are most likely namesakes of George Washington, Thomas Jefferson, John Quincy Adams, Jefferson Davis, James Madison or James Monroe, Andrew Jackson, Oliver Hazard Perry, and James Knox Polk. G. W. could also represent George Whitfield, the Methodist divine in the nineteenth century. L. B. and G. B. were the abbreviations of the male Virginia forenames of Littleberry and Greenberry and spread across the nation. The most popular Europeans to have innumerable American namesakes include Napoleon Bonaparte as in the

example of N. B. Smith. C. C. was for Christopher Columbus, and Victoria in honor of the longest reigning monarch of Great Britain. The popularity of Josephine was introduced into American families in the nineteenth century in honor of the Empress and wife of Napoleon.

Two Revolutionary War figures, William Jasper and John Newton, both of whom served under Francis Marion from South Carolina, had numerous namesakes. Frequently their surnames were combined to yield sons named Jasper, Newton, or Jasper Newton, but such individuals were not descended from either of the pair.

Initials

Many individuals appear in the federal decennial census records with their initials rather than their forenames. This practice was especially widespread in the South following the Civil War. Due to the discrimination against ex-Confederates seeking political office or federal civil positions, southern males resorted to the use of their initials to make any positive identification of their C.S.A. participation much more difficult if not impossible. It was not due to a less conscientious census enumerator.

Renaming of a Living Child

Extending the pedigree of an individual whose forename was changed after birth can be a difficult issue to resolve. Henry Matthew Bockstruck died under his name as reflected in his obituary, death certificate, tombstone, and probate file in 1901 in Montgomery County, Illinois. He had served in the Civil War from Missouri and received a Union pension. He was married under the name of Henry Matthew Bockstruck, and he appeared under that name with his parents, Johann Wilhelm Heinrich and Catharine Maria, nee Brune, Bockstruck in the passenger arrival records at the port of New Orleans, Louisiana on 26 November 1852. He was born 15 January 1837, but he did not appear in the parish register in his native village in Germany.

The Name Is the Game: Onomatology and the Genealogist

There was a confirmation record for a Friedrich Matthias Bockstruck in Borgholzhausen, Westphanlia on 27 April 1851. He was a son of Johann Wilhelm Heinrich and Catharine Maria, nee Brune, Bockstruck. No birth or confirmation record for a Heinrich Mathias Bockstruck was found in the parish register of Borgholzhausen.   Extending his maternal ancestry revealed that his mother was a daughter of Heinrich Matthias Brune who died 17 September 1850. His daughter had not named a son for her father so the family changed the name of their son Friedrich Matthias Bockstruck who was born 15 January 1837 to Heinrich Matthias Bockstruck   in memory of his recently departed maternal grandfather. Since the family immigrated to the United States two years later, every American record had his name as Heinrich Matthias Bockstruck while every German record had his name as Friedrich Matthias Bockstruck.

Chapter 3 Surnames

The use of an additional name to differentiate among people of the same Christian name in a community began as a byname. It was not until that the second name became hereditary that it became a surname.

The first people to adopt more than one name were the Chinese. It was Emperor Fushi who ordered the use of family names in 2832 B.C.

Family names can be grouped according to five categories. One is for surnames derived from toponyms, i.e. places or features of the landscape or of names of actual localities. The Jacob who lived at the edge of the woods would become Jacob at the woods or Jacob Atwood. His neighbor who lived in the agricultural belt of the community might become John Fields. William Hill, Robert Brooks, John Rivers, or Peter Meadows are other examples of people taking a surname from a landscape feature. The Germans and the English have a high incidence of such surnames.

Other surnames are indicative of a trade or occupation such as Smith, Carpenter, Taylor, Shepherd, Teacher, Turner, Cooper, and Wheelwright.

Sometimes people who excelled in particular roles in morality plays acquired surnames from their roles. Sheriff, Duke, King, and Bishop are examples of such.

Still other surnames arose to express relationships. Jeremiah the son of John became Jeremiah Johnson. William the son of Richard became William Richardson, and Richard the son of William became Richard Williamson. Sometimes the suffix "-son" was expressed in the possessive so that the letter "s" was appended to the Christian name as in Williams for the son of William or Harris for the son of Harry.

Sometimes it was the diminutive of a forename which led to the adoption of the surname as in Dickson or Robinson. Patronymical surnames predominate among the Welsh, Scots, Irish, Danes, Swedes, and Norwegians. They are also widespread among the Germans and Poles.

Surnames also derived from nicknames indicating a physical or personality trait such as Goodfellow, Short, or Black. The Italians and Irish favor this category.

It was said of the Todd family of Kentucky that their surname had two d's while God had only one.

Maiden Names

In the British colonies outside of New England, civil records of vital statistics may not have been maintained and religious records may not have survived. When the available court records do not reveal the maiden name of a wife, it could be because she changed her condition but not her surname. William Hastings, the son of Henry Hastings, was born in 1759, married his first cousin, Amey Hastings, 26 October 1785 in Amelia County, Virginia. Her father, William Hastings, gave his consent. Fortunately, the civil marriage record survived to make it possible to identify her maiden name.

Olive Branch married his kinswoman Verlinche Branch in Henrico County, Virginia but no civil or church record exists to prove her maiden name. The bride's forename was one peculiar to the Branch family and was a very good clue for identifying her maiden name.

The Name Is the Game: Onomatology and the Genealogist

Spelling Fixation

It is a mistaken belief that different spellings of a surname applied to people from different families. A good example is Sir Walter Raleigh. His surname became the capital of the state of North Carolina and the seat of Wake County. Another American city named in his honor is Rolla, Missouri although the spelling tends to conceal the connection.

The name of Sir Walter Raleigh has appeared in written records as Raghley, Raghlie, Raileigh, Rale, Raleagh, Raleghe, Raleghus Ralego, Raleigh, Raleighe, Raleile. Raleygh, Ralight, Ralighe, Ralle, Ralleg, Rallleigh, Raughleigh, Raughley, Raughleye, Raughlie, Raughly, Raulaeus, Raule, Rauleghe, Rawligh, Rawlight, Rawlighe, Rawly, Rawlye, Rawlyghe, Raylie, Raylye, Raylygh, Reightly, Reighly, Rauley, Rhaleigh, Rolye, Wrawley, and Wrawly.

In the aftermath of the Civil War George Wise published his work, *The Autograph of William Shakespeare* (Philadelphia: P. E. Abel, 1869) giving 9,000 spelling variations of the most celebrated individual in the history of the English language. No name is lacking in variant spellings and close attention must be paid to all possibilities. Andrew Jackson said a man who could not spell his name more than three ways was not worth knowing, so Shakespeare falls within that criterion.

Surname Confusion

In colonial New Jersey Cornelis Lambertse Cool settled in Somerset County where he appeared in the records under Cool and Kool. In the same county there were English families with the surname of Cole. Since both surnames had the same pronunciation, members of both families used the spelling of the other. In neighboring Amwell in Hunterdon County one finds a German family of Kuhls about 1730. By 1750 they were also using Cool and Kool as their surname. By 1780 They were using the English spelling of their surname. Genealogical research on these families would require careful attention to the surnames in order to extend the pedigree of

The Name Is the Game: Onomatology and the Genealogist

Cool/Kool, Cole, and Kuhl families.

Matthias Sharptnstyn settled in Hunterdon County, New Jersey, prior to 1734. Various members of the family shortened their surname to Sharf, Scarf, or Sharps. Within three generations some of them were using the ultra British surname of Sharpe.

Misinterpretation of Letters of Surnames

Both manuscript sources and their published counterparts may contain entries whose correct version are impossible to discern. The migration of both into databases only compounds the problem. Examples include:

Largent or Sargent	McSorley or McLorley
Gosling or Josling	Tacy or Lacy
Moor or Moon	Tomson or Samson
Burnett and Barnett	Heath or Keath
Jarrett or Jarrell	League or Teague
Prosser or Prossett	Bayley or Bagley
Cocke or Corke	Jordan or Yourdan
Walles or Waller	Farmar or Jarman
Shelton or Skelton	Hunt or Hart
Norton or Horton	Yater or Yates
Mashburn or Washburn	Wisdom or Misdom
Slaton or Stanton	Binns or Burns
Green or Greer	Warren or Warner
Loid or Lord	Gennings or Jennings
Lands or Sands	Matson or Watson
Powl or Paul	Martin or Mortin
Farmer or Turner	Marlin or Martin
Findley or Lindley	

Zimmerman and Timmerman may also fall into this category, although the latter is the Dutch spelling for the former, which is German.

The Name Is the Game: Onomatology and the Genealogist

The Un-aspirated Initial Letter of Surnames

The silent letter "H" can conceal relevant entries in contemporary indexes to legal records such as wills and deeds. Examples include:

Helmes and Elmes
Humphrey and Umphrey
Harrell and Arrell
Harrington and Arrington

Failure to bear this pattern in mind could make it challenging to find a person in relevant records. Anyone seeking to locate a land record for Conrad Hieronymus in Frederick County, Virginia in 1766. By reading all of the records for the appropriate period of time, one would discover that a Conrod Oronimus received a land grant in the Northern Neck in 1766. Simply examining a record group for the correct spelling and known spelling variations could leave a researcher with the mistaken conclusion that the party in question was not there. The same practice may also affect forenames such as Hannah for Anna and Helen for Ellen.

Pronunciations

Pronunciation may be reflected in variant spellings such as Roe and Wroe. If variant spellings occur in the same document, the evidence is overwhelming that in the community involved they were considered to be the same name. In a South Carolina deed James Pollock also appeared as James Polk. In earlier land records he appeared as James Pogue and James Poage. Still earlier generations of the family were recorded as Poack. In Virginia William Hastin also appeared as William Hastings, William Heaston, and William Hasting. In New England the Andros family is also recorded as Andrews, Morey also appeared as Mowry, and Tuttle also appeared as Tutthill.

When someone unfamiliar with a party records his or her name, the spelling can shift to a spelling accommodate the sounds for an entirely different family name. Randall as spoken could replace Randolph, Warrick could replace Warwick, Herod could replace Harwood, and Harrell could replace Harwell. When both spellings appear in the same records over a span of time, it is less and less obvious that both spellings refer to the same family.

One of the more unusual cases of spelling and pronunciation involves the Enroughty family which lived a few miles below Richmond, Virginia. The surnames Enroughty and Darby are synonymous and interchangeable. Darby was not only easier to spell but was also easier to pronounce. They were descendants of Derby Enroughty and used the spelling of Enroughty but pronounced it as Darby. Derby Enroughty, the founder of the family in America, had sons named Derby and John. Each of them in turn named a son John so the two first cousins were differentiated by the use of their father's forename–John Enroughty son of Enroughty and John Enrougthy son of Derby Enroughty. The latter gradually became known as John Derby, but he did not alter the spelling of his surname Enroughty.

Another example involves the Averitt surname, which appeared in the 1790 census as Averat, Averatt, Averet, Averett, Averit, Averite, Avert, and Avret. In Southside Virginia it also appeared as Avery, Avera, and Avory. These variations reflect a lack of standardization of spelling, phonetic variations, and perhaps two distinct surnames which appeared in the same locality allowing for both families to become known by the other's surname.

Alvin Goodenough was of New England stock and settled in the midwest. People unacquainted with the family would undoubtedly vocalize the surname in three syllables: Good e nough. It was actually pronounced "Goode no." Alvin Goodenough appears in one federal census with the spelling of Goodenough. In the following enumeration a decade later he appeared as Goodeno.

The Terminal "G"
Many surnames have the suffix of "-ing" as in Harding. Spoken

English dropped the terminal "g" so that Harding was pronounced Harden. Welding became Weldon, Collings became Collins, and Rushing became Rushen. There is the likelihood that individuals bearing such surnames would appear under both spellings dependent upon whether or not the scribe making the record was the same individual.

Nee, Alias, and Genannt

In the necrology columns in nineteenth century newspapers the French word for born, "nee," was widespread to indicate the maiden names of females. French was the language of international diplomacy and was equated with culture and accounted for the popularity of the use of nee to indicate the maiden name of a female, as in the example of Mary Jane, nee Speed, Briggs.

The Latin "alias" was also used to indicate the maiden name of a female, but it had other uses. In Charles City County, Virginia in 1672 John Roach was recorded as John Roach alias Royster indicating that the two surnames were interchangeable in oral form even though the spellings were not likely to be recognizable to the uniformed. In Albemarle County, Virginia the county clerk in 1756 wrote in a deed Thomas Stevens alias Stephens. The barrister, Charles Carroll, of Maryland left no children. His legatees were the children of his sister, Mary Clare, nee Carroll, MacCubbin. In order to receive their inheritance, Nicholas MacCubbin and his brother, James MacCubbin, legally had their surname changed by act of the legislature. They appeared as James Carroll alias MacCubbin and Nicholas Carroll alias MacCubbin.

Alias can also be indicative of an illegitimate child who could not inherit his father's surname as his own because a bastard had no right to inherit. The child would instead bear his mother's surname. Over time he might appear with his mother's surname alias his father's surname.

The Name Is the Game: Onomatology and the Genealogist

In Orangeburg District, South Carolina the pastor, the Rev. John Giessendanner, reported in the church register the death of a congregant. "On Saturday March 30th 1751 was entered in the church yard of Orangeburg the Body of Gideon Jennings an old Protestant Italian Liver in this township these 14 years past, who died the day before, his age unknown." A few years later in 1756 his widow died, and the burial entry in the church book was "On Friday Sept. 17th died and on Saturday the 18th was Entered in the church yard of Orangeburg the body of Ursula, widow of Gideon Zanini alias Jennings late of Orangeburg deceased aged sixty-seven years." Clearly the family had abandoned their foreign surname for a English one which had no corresponding sound or translation.

Current usage of the term alias is a name assumed by a person as a disguise. John Macey was a runaway servant of William Wyatt of Williamsburg, Virginia, and fled to North Carolina where he used the name of John Murphey in 1738 according to a legal notice in the newspaper.

Genannt is one German equivalent of alias. In certain parts of Germany, e.g. Westphalia, one's surname was the name of the farm which one owned. Johann Heinrich Brune was born 16 July 1744 in Borgholzhausen. His parents were Johann Diedrich and Catharina Ilsabein Brune. A search of the parish register for the marriage of his parents produced no entry for a groom Johann Diedrich Brune to a bride named Catharine Ilsabein. By comparing the forenames of grooms and brides in the parish register, a genealogist located an entry which unlocked the impasse. Johann Diedrich Ostmeyer married Catharine Ilsabein Brune 2 December 1740. His wife was an heiress to realty. When she inherited the family farm, he moved into her home and took her surname as his. He was Johann Diedrich Brune genant Ostmeyer at the birth and baptism of their first child. The genant designation did not appear in any subsequent baptismal entries of their children, all of whom bore the Brune surname. If he had died and his widow married another man named Johann Diedrich, there would have been no discernible clue in the baptismal entries in the parish register so all entries for the appropriate period of time would need to be read. Other German synonyms for genannt include nunc and forn.

Adoption of a Step-parent's Surname

Thomas Jackson Greenwood of Newton, Massachusetts became an orphan in his infancy. Alexander Shepard oversaw his education and had no son of his own so Thomas Jackson Greenwood alias Shephard assumed the name of his benefactor in 1781.

Jonathan Singletary born 17 January 1639/40 in Salisbury, Massachusetts spent his childhood in Haverhill, Massachusetts. He later removed to Woodbridge, New Jersey where he was known as Jonathan Dunham. His heirs in a document dated in 1703 referred to themselves as Dunham alias Singletary stating that their father was the son of Richard and Susannah Singletary.

Military Influence on Surnames

Anton Diedrick was a Belgian who had been shanghaied in his native Antwerp and sent to sea. He eventually made his escape at the American port of Galveston in Texas in 1846. He had no means of support, and a couple of recruiting soldiers of the U.S. Army for the Mexican War convinced him that if he would make his mark on the enlistment paper, he would be fed and cared for. Since he spoke Flemish only, he was unable to respond to the question of what his name was. Receiving no reply, one of the enlisting soldiers in exasperation said, "Aw, he's Dutch all over. We'll call him that." His new forename, Dutchallover, proved to be too cumbersome, and in due course it was shortened to Dutchover.

It was considered patriotic for an American to hire a substitute to take his place in military service from the colonial era to the Civil War. Sometimes the substitute served under the name of his sponsor rather than his own identity. In the Revolutionary War Ebenezer Conant of Connecticut swore that he answered to the name of Bibbens while he was in the service. John Cooper of New York stated that his substitute served under his name.

Baron Gustavus Heinrich von Wetter Rosendahl was from Estonia and a subject of the czar of Russia when he came to North America to fight in the Revolutionary War. He was born 1 January 1753, and died 26 June 1829. He outlived his spouse and all of his children. His daughter, the Baroness von Mohrenschildt, left issue. Afterwards he wrote "But as the issue of an opposition to the power of Great Britain was dubious and the attempt rather venturous, I thought it advisable to call myself by the first four letters of my proper name, viz. Rose, by the name of John Rose." He served in the 7th Pennsylvania Regiment as a surgeon's mate from 1777 to 1783. Most of his military records carried his name as John Rose. In addition to his *nom de guerre* he also had still another alias, John Henderson.

From English to Another Language
Within North America were colonies of other European powers including Spain, France, Sweden, and the Netherlands. People leaving the English-speaking jurisdictions might have their surnames Galicized or Hispanicized. The Irish surnames of O'brien and Murphy became Obregon and Murfi in the Spanish possessions. Santiago Buy in Mexican Texas was James Bowie back in the United States.

From One European Language to Another
In Louisiana were colonial Germans whose surnames were Galicized. Miltenberger became Mil de Bergue. Schantz became Chance, Zweig became Le Branche, Vogt became Foque, Buerckel became Percle, Rommel became Rome, Wehrle became Verlay, and Schletter became Chelaitre.

In the 16th and 17th centuries in Europe many individuals adopted the Latin counterpart of their surname so that a German Muller would have become a Molitor, a Schaefer would have become a Pastorius, and a Schwarzerde would have become a Melanthon.

In Southwest Louisiana in the Roman Catholic Church at Opelousas is the baptism of Marie Jeansonne on 7 January 1803. Hers was an adult baptism. She was 30 years of age. She was identified as the spouse of Robert Barrow and the daughter of Daniel Jeansonne and Susanne Daly. Most importantly, she was reported to have been born in North Carolina. Her surname in French Louisiana and her origin in North Carolina eliminated any French ancestry for her and provided the clue that one should seek records about her early life under the English version of her surname–Johnson.

If an American scribe who created a record involving a French speaking Louisianan had no knowledge of French, he might have written Terry for Teriot. Perot for Peryoux, or Como for Comeaux.

On 10 August 1703, during the War of the Spanish Succession, there was a surprise Indian attack on the English settlement of Wells, Maine. The band of Indians took as hostages Martha (Lord) Littlefield and her three children, Aaron, Ruth, and Tabitha. Tabitha became a squaw of one of her captors, but the French were able to ransom two of her children, Aaron and Ruth Littlefield. Ruth entered a convent where her surname appeared at Ledril. Aaron Littlefield, who had been born 20 October 1694,was baptized a Roman Catholic at Bourcheville 27 January 1704 and given the French name of Pierre Augustin Littrefils. Littrefils had not existed as a surname in New France up until that time and camouflaged his Hampshire, England ancestry.

Before the United States acquired the Louisiana Purchase in 1803, there was an inhabitant in Missouri named John Philip Gates. Considerable research suggested that he was not from any Gates family in cis-Mississippi America. He was noted for his facility of Indian languages so it seemed worthwhile to investigate his having come into the area from the Upper Mississippi Valley or the St. Lawrence River Valley. Eventually a document was uncovered revealed that he was actually the son of Philip Goetz from Basel, Switzerland, and who had settled in Quebec. The son adopted the spelling of the similarly sounding surname of Gates.

Young is a surname from the British Isles and found in a Southside colonial Virginia family. There were three brothers named Thomas Young, LeGros Young, and Francis Young. Earlier they had a double surname of Thomas Cadet Young, LeGros Cadet Young, and Francis Cadet Young. Their father was a Huguenot colonist, Michael Cadet, whose surname in English meant the younger. He was known as Michael Cadet Young.

The Dit Name
The French word "dit" can be translated as "called" or "known as."

There were some 10,000 French colonists who came to New France in North America in the eighteenth century. The practice of the dit name was extremely common in the French army, and many of the French saw military duty in New France. After they completed their military service, many of them chose to remain in North America. There were relatively few different surnames among them, and there was even a more limited number of forenames. The result was that there were numerous individuals with the same forename and same surname. Dit names provided a solution in differentiating among such individuals. Families also used double or triple surnames. The French added a sobriquet to their surname and in some instances ceased to use their family surname and became known by their sobriquet. Alexandre Lacoste dit Languedoc was a native of Languedoc, a province in France. Accordingly, members of the family appeared as Lacoste, Lacoste dit Languedoc, Lacoste-Languedoc, or Languedoc. Their sobriquet reflected the family's geographical origins.

The Name Is the Game: Onomatology and the Genealogist

A dit name could also reflect a personality trait, an occupation, or a physical characteristic, The sobriquet can be helpful in unsorting members of various branches of the family. It also makes known that direct male line descendants exist with different surnames.

Three sons of Giles Chauvin of Montreal settled in the Illinois country about 1735. His son, Louis Chauvin, used only the family name. Another son was known as Joseph Chauvin dit Charleville for a place. The third brother was Philippe Chauvin who died young leaving a son who was known as Francois Chauvin dit Joyeuse for a personality trait. His descendants anglicized his dit name to Joyce. The outcome was that people bearing the surnames Chauvin, Charleville, and Joyce share the same male line descent.

Dialects and Minorities
The Sorbs or Wends were a Slavic people from southeastern Germany in the Spree River Valley of Saxony many of whom immigrated to the United States. These Lusatian Sorbs had their own language and resisted assimilation into neighboring German communities both in Europe and in the United States. Their surnames were rendered differently from Sorbian to German and may conceal their true identity.

Sorbian	German
Cyz	Aiesch
Domaska	Domaschke
Hola	Hohle
Hornik	Hornig
Hurban	Urban
Kokel	Krockel
Kowar	Schmidt
Krawc, Krawz	Schneider
Krizan	Zieschang

The Name Is the Game: Onomatology and the Genealogist

Nemc	Niemz
Pjech	Pech
Rjenc	Rentsch
Smoler	Schmaler
Wicaz	Lehmann
Wjela	Wehle

A christening record might have the name of the babe as Agnes Sperling in German. Her marriage record might have her name as Hainscha Wrobel in Wendish.

German surnames can also have different dialectal spellings. The colonial American German family of Segaesser from Waldsheim also appeared in the local records in Germany as Sensinger. The two spellings reflect the Swiss origin of the family and the local German dialect. The immigrant, Ulrich Segaesser or Ulrich Sensinger, appeared under both spellings in the Old World and in colonial America. The two surnames were interchangeable.

There were also spelling differences between Hochdeutsch and Plattdeutsch, or High German and Low German. While the Low German Jacob Cleinen closely resembles the High German Jacob Klenin and Johann Heinrich Kleentrup resembles Johann Heinrich Klendrub, the Low German Hans Korte is less readily recognizable as Johann Kurze in High German.

Dutch Surnames

The Dutch in New Netherland practiced a patronymic naming pattern so that a man's sons had a surname composed of the father's forename plus the suffix of "-sen." Hendrick Jansen had a son who was named Pieter Hendricksen who in turn had a son named Hendrick Pietersen.

Arent Prall of Staten Island usually appeared as Arent Janszen, which was his patronymic. He relocated to New Paltz where his trade was that of

The Name Is the Game: Onomatology and the Genealogist

a wheelwright, so he appeared as Arent Rademaaker or Arent de Ramaacher. Cornelis Van Hoorn was a fisherman and sometimes used the name of Cornelis Vischer.

Claes Janse also appeared under variant spellings of his patronymic as Claes Jansen and Claes Janszen. He married as Claes Janszen van Purmerendt. Claes was a diminutive of Nicholas, and Janszen was his patronymic. Van Purmeredt was his place of origin. When he came to New Netherland, he was a wheelwright and appeared on the passenger arrival list as Claes Jansen vanpurmerent Ramaker. He later became a cooper or barrel maker and was buried as Claes Janszen Kuyper.

When the English seized possession of New Netherland, their officials insisted that the Dutch choose one surname and use it thereafter for themselves and their descendants. They were not necessarily successful because the Dutch pattern of surname fluidity persisted even into the middle of the eighteenth century.

Abbreviations of Surnames
David Williamson might appear as David Wmson and Hezekiah Robertson might appear as Hezekiah Robtson.

While the concept is rather easy to grasp, the paper trail can be deceptively complex as in the case of Conrad Pennypacker.

The Pennebecker family was established in the eighteenth century in Pennsylvania where it became Pennypacker. According to John H. Gwathmey, *Historical Register of Virginians in the Revolution Soldiers, Sailors, Marines 1775-1783* (Baltimore, Md.: Genealogical Publishing Co., Inc. 1973), p. 616, Conrad Pennypacker served as a Fife Major in the 3rd and 4th Virginia Regiments of the Continental Line. He also appeared as Pennybacker and Penybaker in the same units. In addition he appeared with the same rank in the same units as Conrad Pennybacer. He also appeared under the latter spelling in the 8th and 12th Regiments. According to Gaius Marcus Brumbaugh, *Revolutionary War Records Virginia* (Baltimore, Md.: Genealogical Publishing Co., Inc. 1995), pp. 194 & 368, Virginia bounty land warrant number #8206 was issued to William Pennybaker for Conrod Pennybacker's service as a Fife Major.

Virginia Military Records (Baltimore, Md.: Genealogical Publishing Co., Inc., 1983), pp. 682 & 684 indicated that Coonrod Pennybacer, Fife Major, of the 4th Regiment was paid £3.2.6 on 14 April 1778 for the previous March. He was in a detachment from different regiments under Captain Burnley and Lt. Samuel Gill on their march to headquarters.

Sarah Pennybaker, the wife of Conrad Pennybaker, received one hundred pounds of pork and two barrels of corn from the county court in Berkeley County, Virginia on 22 November 1780 while her husband was away in the service. Lloyd de Witt Bockstruck, *Revolutionary War Pensions Awarded by State Governments 1775-1784, the General and Federal Governments Prior to 1814, and by Private Acts of Congress to 1905.* (Baltimore, Md.: Genealogical Publishing Company, 2011), p. 628.

According to Louis A. Burgess's *Virginia Soldiers of 1776* (Baltimore, Md.: The Clearfield Company, 1973), I, 397, on 9 February 1828 in Council, it was advised that the heirs of Conrad Pennybaker be allowed land bounty as a Fife Major in the Continental Line. On 6 December 1817, at Union Town Pennsylvania, Jacob P. Baker stated that his father Conrad Pennybaker was a Fife Major in the 4th Regiment and died during the war in 1775 [sic]. The son appointed Samuel Smith his attorney. Smith acknowledged the power of attorney in Fayette County, Pennsylvania before Jonathan Rowland, Justice of the Peace.

Jacob Johnston and John Fitzgerald deposed that they were well acquainted with Jacob P. Baker and certified as to his signature. Samuel Smith of Union Township, Fayette County, Pennsylvania as attorney for

The Name Is the Game: Onomatology and the Genealogist

Jacob Penny Baker, the only heir of Conrad P. Baker, deceased, appointed Mr. George W. Mumford his attorney in fact and acknowledged same before David H. Sharrard, J. P. Bounty land Warrant #6717 for 400 acres was issued 31 March 1828.

According to Virgil D. White, *Index to Revolutionary War Service Records* (Waynesville, Tenn.: The National Historical Publishing Company, 1995), I, 98 and III, 2103, Conrad P. Baker served as a fife major in the 4th Virginia Regiment of the Continental Line as well as the 3rd Regiment and in the 4th, 8th, and 12th Regiments. He also appeared as Conrad Pennnebaker, Conrod Pennibaker, Conrad Pennebaker, Conrod Pennybacer, Conrad Pennebaker, Coenrad Pennybaker, and Coonrod Pennebaker. His compiled military service record in the National Archives revealed that he served under Captains Isaac Beall, John Stith, and George Walls, and Colonels Thomas Eliott and Robert Lawson. He enlisted from Berkeley County, Virginia for three years, and his payroll records survived from May 1777, all of 1778, and to November 1779. He was at Valley Forge, Camp Paramus, Carrel's ferry, White Plains, Robertson's farm, Middlebrook, Smith Clove, Ramapough, Haverstraw, and Morristown during the course of the war.

Conrad Pennybaker's unit was at Charleston, South Carolina, when the city fell to the British. It would seem that Conrad Pennybaker–perhaps in order to be released from detention– enlisted in the British forces and served as a Loyalist. According to Murtie June Clark, *Loyalists in the Southern Campaign of the Revolutionary War* (Baltimore, Md.: Genealogical Publishing Co., Inc., 1981), I, 56, 437-439, Conrad Pennybaker was a drummer in the King's Rangers under Maj. James Wright. He was paid for service from 24 February to 21 April 1781, 24 April 1781 to 24 June 1781, 25 October 1781 to 24 December 1781, and 25 April 1782 to 24 June 1782.

When the British forces evacuated Savannah, he sailed to Jamaica

The Name Is the Game: Onomatology and the Genealogist

with other British Loyalists and Tories. According to Sandra Riley in her work *Homeward Bounty: A History of the Bahama Islands to 1850 with a Definitive Study of Abaco in the American Loyalist Plantation Period* (Miami, Fla.: Island Research, 1983), pp. 157, 194, 197, 273, & 275, Conrad Pennybaker changed his name to Conrad P. Baker and was a Georgia Loyalist and drummer in the King's Rangers. He had come from Georgia to East Florida. He had a grant for 80 acres from Lord Dunmore in 1789 at Guyana Cay in and around Spencer's Bight in the Bahamas.

In 1802 he and others gave warning to all persons cruising about the island not to land at Great Cay under any pretense. He had one slave named Ginny or Jenny. In 1828 he gave gifts of land to his wife Margaret, his son Philip, and his daughter Nancy. He also gave his son a seventeen foot boat which he had built with his own hands in 1825. His land had escheated by 1834 due to the failure of the heirs to pay the quit rents on the land. The slave register for that year indicated that Conrad P. Baker had one slave and one field.

The Virginia Land Office Military Certificates, Microfilm Roll 27, PE-PO has two folders for Conrad Pennybaker who was a fife major in the Continental Line. Bounty Land Warrant #6717 for 400 acres was issued to his heir, his son Jacob P. Baker, on 31 March 1828. Jacob P. Baker stated that his father enlisted in 1775 and died in the service. The son had given a power of attorney to Samuel Smith to obtain what he was due. Jacob P. Baker was from Fayette County, Pennsylvania.

The other bounty land file was submitted by William Panabaker of Miami County, Ohio who appointed his son, Adam Pannabaker, of Horton's Gap, Culpeper County, Virginia his attorney in order to receive what he might be due. He stated that he was the brother and heir of Conrad Pennybaker who had enlisted for three years, served under Capt. George Walls, and died intestate in the service. He stated that he spelled his surname differently than his brother, Conrad. He received warrant #8006 for

400 acres.

It would seem that Conrad Pennybaker opted to leave the United States at the end of the war rather than return home because he had betrayed his country and was perhaps subject to retaliation. He may have also found it more expedient to abandon his wife and child. Since he never returned home after the war, his widow and child seemingly concluded that he had died in the service.

This example typifies the permutations in the spelling and the necessity of becoming immersed in records, recognizing what the records do and do not reveal, and that all possibilities need to be considered and thoroughly investigated. His paper trail revealed that Pennybaker was also spelled Pennabaker.

The Crossed Tail of the Letter P
In seventeenth century English a cross bar through the tail of the letter "p" was a standard abbreviation for "per" , "par", or "pur". Accordingly to the untrained researcher Harper could be rendered incorrectly as Harp and Carper as Carp. Coop and Hoop were actually Cooper and Hooper, but published transcripts or abstracts may not have discerned this archaic letter form.

The Long "S"
Until the middle of the nineteenth century both handwritten and printed works made use of a character representing the letter "S" which to the untrained eye resembles the letter "f" or "p". Accordingly, the surname Cass might be misinterpreted as Cape. One inexperienced genealogist thought that her ancestor was Jepe Mope born in Tennepee. He was actually Jesse Moss born in Tennessee.

The Female Title of Mrs.
In the colonial period a female from a prominent family would have

been recorded with the title, Mrs. It bore no indication of marital status as it does today. When Mrs. Sarah Randolph referred to John Corbin as her father-in-law in a document, she was appearing under her birth name, and John Corbin was actually her step-father. She had never been married. There was still another interpretation of the title Mrs. Prior to World War II among England's great landed families, the use of Mrs. applied to housekeepers and head cooks on the staff of the aristocracy and nobility with no indication of marital status although the bearer could also have been married.

Idem Sonans

The legal principle of *idem sonans* indicates that names are considered to be same even though the spellings are not identical but the pronunciation is. If a warrant were issued for the arrest of John Lawrence and he was taken into custody and brought before the King's bench, he could have requested that the case against him be dismissed because the writ for his arrest bore his name as John Laurance when everyone in his community knew he was known as John Lawrence. If it were not for the principle of *idem sonans*, he would have been a free man.

The German surname of Bach tends to be recorded in colonial Pennsylvania with the spelling of Baugh which is the Ulster Scot spelling for the surname. The same name could also be written phonetically in English as Baff.

The surnames of Bankston, Bankson, and Pinkston are variants of the New Sweden family whose surname was actually Bengtsson. The surname of Swanson also derives from Swenson. The New Sweden surname of Romppainen is common among the Varmland Finns in Sweden and became Rambo in America.

Matthias Warner [sic] Baker married Neomi Bates on the 16th day of April in 1789 in Lyme, Connecticut. The vital records of the town record the births of their eight children: Matthias Baker 7 born April 1790, Mary Baker 2 December 1791, Sophia Baker 6 May 1793, Elizabeth Baker 11 April 1795, John Herman Baker 9 July 1796, Lucy Baker 15 February 1798, George Herron Baker 10 April. 1799, and Catherine Baker 21 February 1801. An alert genealogist noted that it was unusual at that period of time for a person to have two forenames and that Matthias was somewhat unusual as a forename in English-speaking families. The English equivalent, Matthew, would more likely have been used. Both sons bore double forenames, and an examination of the original town record revealed that the rendering of the second forename of the younger son was actually George Herman in the original and not George Herron. These forenames would also be common in German, and the daughters Sophia and Catherine bore forenames which might also suggest a German origin. In addition Warner was not a name found in any other family in the town. The records of Connecticut men in the militia during the War of 1812 revealed that one Mathias Wisenbaker served as a private under Asa Copeland from 14 Sept. 1813 to 1 Nov. 1813. Clearly Wisenbaker was the correct surname.

For someone well acquainted with American colonial families, the surname of Wisenbaker would be recognized as a German family which settled among the Salzburgers in Georgia, although they themselves were not Salzburgers. Members of the family were mariners and involved with commerce with New England. Lyme, Connecticut is a coastal town so it would be reasonable that a Georgia German could become a New England Yankee.

Pearl Rahn Gann, *Georgia Salzburgers and Allied Families* (Greenville, S.C.: Southern Historical Press, 2003), IV, 3205 & 3243, stated that Mathias Wisenbaker moved from Savannah to New London, Connecticut before 1804. His children were Mathias, Jr., Mary, Sophia, Elizabeth, John Herman, Lucy who married Elijah Herrick, George Herman, and Catherine who married Jacob Holmes.

The Name Is the Game: Onomatology and the Genealogist

William Baldwin made his will in Amelia County, Virginia, 14 April 1755 and named his wife Susannah Baldwin, son John Baldwin, grandson William Baldwin, daughter Elizabeth the wife of James Davis, grandson George Baldwin, grandson John Davis, grandson William Davis, Mary Bennitt wife of Benjamin Bennitt, Benjamin Baldwin, and Sarah the wife of John Roberts. A genealogist was interested in Sarah Roberts and wanted to establish that she was indeed a daughter of the testator. The index to Virginia probate records prior to 1800 did not reveal any other probate records in Amelia County for someone with the surname of Baldwin. A page by page search of the will books of Amelia County seemed to be the next step in the research process. One Susannah Bolding made her will in Amelia County, 7 February 1770. She named her son-in-law, William Bennett, her son Benjamin Bolding, her daughter Elizabeth Davis, her daughter Sarah Roberts, and her granddaughter, Sarah Bennett. The legatees in the two wills demonstrate that the same family was involved. The difference in spelling of the testator and testatrix was due to the fact Susannah Baldwin was illiterate and to the fact that the one who wrote her will was seemingly not acquainted with the spelling of her surname. He rendered the document using the pronunciation. Baldwin and Bolding were names with the same sound. In 1727 William Baldwin had received two land grants in neighboring North Carolina where the scribe used the spelling of Bolding for his surname.

Sometimes the pronunciation of a surname is no longer obvious but has evolved into a totally different pronunciation with different spellings. Grimes and Graham were formerly identically pronounced and were interchangeable. This principle may or may not be explanation for the family of Israel and Rachel Heald of Stow, Massachusetts. The births of their children were recorded with the same surname: twins John and Israel on 15 October 1714, Rachel 18 February 1717, and twins Mary and Samuel 2 April 1714. When Rachel died in 1747, her surname was recorded as Hale. Their son, Samuel Hale, died at Leominster, Massachusetts, in 1805. Hale continued as the spelling of the surname among later generations.

The Name Is the Game: Onomatology and the Genealogist

The Crenshaw family of Virginia also appeared as Granger. On 25 December 169[?] Thomas Cranshaw, the son of Thomas Cranshaw, was baptized in St. Peter's Parish in New Kent County. On 21 January 1699/1700 Elizabeth Granger, the daughter of Thomas Granger, was baptized. The lack of awareness of this practice would prevent reconstituting a family.

The French Huguenot family of Guillaume Fouquet became William Fuqua in Virginia. It is indicative of a surname from a language other than English which, although it retains the pronunciation, undergoes a spelling metamorphosis. The surname of Tacket is actually the French surname of Tacquet.

Other examples include:

Burroughs and Burrus	Royal and Rial
Hobart and Hubbard	Taylor and Tyler
Briggs and Bridges	Sartin and Certain
Lovell and Lovewell	Kaufman and Coughman
Maury and Murray	Vreland and Freland
Hawthorne and Horton	Stockton and Stogden
Gooch and Gouge	Bidwell and Bridwell
Crownover and Couvenhoven	Pierce and Purse
Childress and Childers	Kerr and Carr
Strayhorn and Strong	Rieves and Reeves
Blount and Blunt	Herod and Harwood
Randolph and Randall	Knowland , Nowland/Nolin
Doty and Doubty or Doughty	Neighbors and Nabors
Kneal or Neil of Nihell	Wroe and Roe
Mayberry and Mabry	St. Maur and Semour
Routh and Ruth	Prather and Prator
Nochs and Knox	Bernard and Barnett
Graff and Grove	Burwell and Burrill
Diel and Deal or Teal	Callowhill and Carroll

The Name Is the Game: Onomatology and the Genealogist

Pfeil and File

Gawin and Gowon

Schoen and Shane

Ironmonger and Monger

Timberlake and Timberlag

Michaux and Missher

Napier and Napper

Norsworthy and Nazary

Piggot and Picket

Seawell and Sowel

Drewry and Druitt

Rains and Reigns

Gascoigne and Gaskins

Meacham and Mitchem

Beverage and Beveridge

Mickeberry and

Thatcher and Thacker

Mickelburrough

Hollandsworth and Hollingsworth

Gresham and Grissum

Heinsall and Henshaid

Greaton and Graydon

Ware and Weir

Cowper and Cooper

Bressey and Bracy

Lance and Lantz

Cannon and Kennon

Owens and Ownings

Belin and Blaine

Horry and Oury

Colelough and Cokely

Wehrle and Worley

Kay and Key

Quite frequently the same surname with possible spelling variations might not be anticipated or recognized unless it appears in the same record under both spellings. Woodis would not likely be considered by the reader as a variation for Woodhouse unless both versions appeared in the same document, and Bible would not seem to be the alternative English rendering of the German Biebel. Kite is the pronunciation of the surname of Knight in southern parts of the United States.

If the scribe creating the record was unfamiliar with the person whose name he is recording, he would most likely use the spelling of the pronunciation, and over time the phonetic spelling replaces the older correct spelling.

In colonial Virginia the surname of Featherstonehaugh was pronounced as though it were written Fanshaw. In the South the surname of McEachern was the pronunciation of McCann, and the former supplanted the latter spelling.

St. Clair had a pronunciation which approximated the spelling of Sinclair. Another spelling version was Sinkler. Singclear was still another.

In languages such as German sounds may be represented by different letters in English. The "B" and "P" account for Samuel Bentz who might also be written as Samuel Pense. William Brobst might have appeared as William Probst. The letters "B" and "V" were also similar sounds so that Weber becomes Weaver, Stover became Stober, and Huber became Hoover.

The letters "C" and "K" account for Kohlman becoming Coleman, Kaufman becoming Coughman, and Klock becoming Clock. "K" and "G" account for Krummel and Grummel and for Klock and Glock. "D" and "T" were interchangeable so that Hoettel became Huddle and Darter became Tarter. The letters "J" and "Y" account for Joder and Yoder and Jaeger and Yeager.

The terminal vowels "e" and "i' in German, as in Hirschi, Schnebeli, and Schelle, produced Hershey, Snavely and Shelley in English. Eberli became Everley and Stehli became Staley.

In the Thuringian area of German there was a limited pool of names. In order to differentiate between individuals of the same name, people resorted to a beinamen, or nickname, which followed the surname as in the following example:
Max Mueller
Armin Mueller Mops
Fernando Mueller Mops Meister
Elias Mueller Mops Meister Fernando Ballert.
Ignorance of this practice in that region of Germany would mislead one into viewing the beinamen as the surname since it came at the end of a person's

name.

While it is apparent that Ray, Rae, Rhea, Reigh, and Wray are variant spellings of the same surname, the spelling of Reaugh is less likely to come to mind. One good list of such variants is *Surnames Listed in the 1790 United States Census* (Orting, Wash.: Heritage Quest, 198?) with more than 5,700 examples.

In the 1850 census of Pike County, Alabama was a Catrett family in which the older members gave their place of nativity as North Carolina. None of the earlier census indexes of the Tar Heel State, however, included anyone of that surname. There was, moreover, no one of that surname in the index to the state's marriage records. John Catrett had married in Pike County in 1844. None of the Pike County records seems to provide a clue to extending his pedigree. One source indicated that he was a veteran of the War of 1812, so he might have applied and qualified for a federal bounty land grant for his service. Indeed, he did appear as such in a compilation of soldiers in Alabama. The compiler of the work included the deposition John Catrett made when he applied for his federal bounty land. He made his mark so he was illiterate. The clerk styled him John Cartwright alias Cartrett aged 70 years. That clue enabled one to determine that he came from Brunswick County, North Carolina. He had a different accent than many of his Alabama neighbors who created the records of Pike County pertaining to him.

Jacob Cromer was from colonial German stock in South Carolina. His son appeared as Jacob Cromeans and was born *ca.* 1799 in North Carolina. He joined the western migration and settled in Tennessee and later in Alabama. Jacob Cromeans had a son born, *ca.* 1824, in Alabama who became known as Lindsay Cummins. The change was due to the fact that the letter "r" in the surname was silent.

The surname of Banker in America may actually be the English

The Name Is the Game: Onomatology and the Genealogist

version of the German surname, Boenker, because the pronunciation is the same. The German surname of Tschudi becomes Judy in English, and Heinrich Danz becomes Henry Dance. While Winchell is an English surname, it could have become the substitute of the German surname Wuenschel. Doubt is the English rendering of the German Daudt as Nair is for Nehr, Price is for Preiss, Sourwine for Sauerwein, Surface for Zerfass, Swope for Schwab, and Trout for Traudt.

Johannes Meckendorfer appeared on the passenger arrival list of the *Allen* at the port of Philadelphia in 1729. His descendants in the Shenandoah Valley became McInturfer or McInterfeer because Ulster Scots were the ones who generated the court records and gave him an Ulster Scot identity. The Gaelic appearing surname of McEndollar was actually the German Mechenthaler.

Other examples of German surnames assuming an English language origin include:

Betz	Bates
Huth	Hood
Schmal	Small
Uhl	Ewell
Lamm	Lamb
Hauck	Hawk
Whei	Way
Loest	Laced
Niedt	Neat
Hsia	Shaw
Kuhle	Cooley
Bohn	Bowen
Hug	Huck
Schock	Jack
Biehn	Bean
Stihl	Steel

The Name Is the Game: Onomatology and the Genealogist

Guthman   Goodman

In the first quarter of the twentieth century in Lincoln County, North Carolina, descendants of a colonial German progenitor named Klein held a family reunion. In addition to descendants who appeared under that name, direct male line descendants also appeared as Cline, Short, Small, and Little, all of which were English equivalents.

Jacques Hebert might appear in records in Louisiana as Jacques Ebert because the initial letter of his surname was silent. It would not be likely for a researcher, however, to expect him to be found as Jockey Bear in a record made by a English speaking census enumerator who had no knowledge of French. The Scotsman, Hugh Montgomery, was enumerated as Human Gomery in South Carolina, but finding him through any index would not likely meet with any success. These literal verbal equivalents are apparent only when they appeared in an actual record and are spoken orally by the reader.

One researcher seeking to extend a Bird family pedigree had been alert to collect data on individuals who appeared in the records as Byrd and Burd. Unsuccessful, he consulted a compilation of compiled military service records for Confederate soldiers from the state of North Carolina because he was aware that the editors had included references to alternative spellings. He learned that another possibility for Byrd which he had overlooked, was Baird. He repeated his search of the records but was still unsuccessful. He resorted to reading the census records entry by entry. He concentrated on the forenames of the members of the households and pronounced aloud each surname. He was eventually successful. The census enumerator had entered the family as Boyd. The mistake could have been due to the accent of the family member who furnished the data or to what the enumerator heard and recorded.

A good example in Spanish involves Visente Tavar who could also have appeared as Bisente Tabar. Carlos Jimenes might also have been written as Carlos Ximenez or Carlos Gimenez. Another Spanish surname with different initial letter variables is Sepeda, Zepeda, and Cepade.

The English surname of Ratcliffe might appear as Ratley, and Crossland might appear as Crosley.

Translation into English

Many Americans bear a surname which is English in spelling even though the family's heritage was from a different ethnicity. Examples from German surnames include:

Fruehling	Spring
Stein	Stone
Liebe	Love
Klein	Little
Grunewald	Greenwood
Koenig	King
Jung	Young
Freund	Friend
Fuchs	Fox
Schloss	Castle
Glocke	Bell
Stolzfuss	Proudfoot
Koch	Cook
Zimmerman	Carpenter
Jaeger	Hunter
Gerber	Tanner
Bauer	Farmer
Fehrer	Fair
Zahn	Zane
Schmidt	Smith
Schwartz	Black

The Name Is the Game: Onomatology and the Genealogist

One should consult a surname dictionary for any clues of ethnic origins and translations which might be of assistance in extending a pedigree. The entry for the surname of Turnipseed in *The Dictionary of American Family Names,* by Patrick Hanks, indicates that it entered the English language as the translation of the German surname of Rubsamen. A genealogist working with a Texas Turnipseed family was successful in extending the family's pedigree back to Mississippi and earlier still into South Carolina at which point there was an impasse. Knowing that the surname was originally Rubsamen offered the clue to making the bridge from the English translation to the original German that happened in South Carolina. Thereafter it was necessary to follow the German form of the surname. Another example of seemingly English appearing surname is that of Beanblossom. It does not occur in the English language outside of colonial America because it is a translation of the German Bohnenblust.

The English form of a surname might involve several steps. Jacob Heitersbach was baptized 11 Apr. 1706 in Niederbieber, Germany. He was one of the Palatine children brought to the colony of New York under the program of Gov. Hunter. As Jacob Oysterberk, a three-year old orphan, he was bound out to John Williams of Fairfield, Connecticut. He lived in Fairfield, and his offspring were in Westport, Connecticut. Over time the surname evolved into Oysterbanks, O'Banks, O. Banks, and finally emerged as Banks.

The Huguenot refugee, Philip L'Anglois, took the surname of England in Salem, Massachusetts because it was the English translation of his French surname. Andrew and Mary Winter settled in Ashburnham, Worcester County, Massachusetts about the time of the French and Indian War. The town records contain entries for the births of their children Philip 11 March 1754, John 1 March 1756, Jacob 21 October 1758, Andrew 28 March 1761, Mary 24 August 1763, Margaret 19 April 1766, and Kata who was baptized 13 August 1769. Kata was recorded in the town records as a child of Andrew and Mary Windrow on 19 July 1769, and that was the spelling of the surname thereafter.

Surname Shortening
Longer surnames with a suffix which could also be a surname itself have the tendency to be abbreviated in records in such a fashion that the suffix becomes the family name.

John DeLong would become John D. Long. James DeSpain would become James D. Spain or James Dspain, William Arrowsmith would become William A. Smith, and Robert Basbeach would become Robert B. Beach. Seth Pettypool would become Seth Ppoole or Seth Poole. Charles Chaneywolf would become Charles C. Wolf. John Essman would become John S. Mann, William Elmore would become William L. More, Hezekiah Seawright would become Hezekiah C. Wright. Samuel DeForest would become Samuel D. Forest. Peter Seabury might be recorded as Peter C. Bury. John Broadhurst would become John B. Hurst. Jeremiah Highsmith would become Jeremiah H. Smith. Thomas Youngblood would become Thomas Y. Blood and eventually Thomas Blood. Finding a cluster of families with the same middle initial in a locality oftentimes is suggestive of surname shortening.

The Letters "R" and "L"
The sounds of these two letters are identical in many languages. It is exemplified in the diminutive of the forename of Mary–Molly. Palmer might be written as Parmer. Kirkpatrick might be Kilpatrick. Casey might be Kersey. William Elmore might appear as William Alma.

The "r" can be inserted in the oral version of a surname or interchanged with the consonant "n." Thomas Lockett was the progenitor of a seventeenth century Virginia family. His grandson migrated to North Carolina where he was known as Lockheart. Wilkinson would become Wilkerson, Robinson would become Robertson, Cornwell would become Conwell, and Dickinson would become Dickerson. Sawtell would become

The Name Is the Game: Onomatology and the Genealogist

Sartell, Semple would become Sarmple, Hannah would become Hannar, and Matthews would become Marthews. Travis would become Traverse. Causon or Cawson could be variants of Carson. The Irish surname of McDonough would have been spoken as though spelled as McDunner. In some instances both consonants are retained in the surname, e.g. Neathery and Neatherly.

The "r" produces Ivory out of Ivy, Lejurne out of Lejune, Nunnery out of Nunnelly, Sandridge out of Sandidge, Morfitt out of Moffit, Thomerson out of Thomason, Parsel out of Pasel, Fortner out of Faulkner, and Linkcorn out of Lincoln. If the consonant "r" was not in the written form of the name, it was inserted in the spoken version as in George Warshington.

The intrusive "r" can also give rise to a new surname. Meadows, for example, could become Meaders. Tobert is a variation of Talbott.

"Ou" and "Wh"
The farther north one goes in Great Britain, the more likely is the possibility that the unaspirated "Wh" becomes "Ou" so that Whitefall would become Quitfall, and Worsham and Washam would become Ouslim.

Gender and Surnames
The taufschein or birth and baptismal certificate of the daughter of Jacob Meyer and his wife Susannah, geboren Beitlerin, states their daughter Maria was born on 8 September 1819 in Springfield Township in Bucks County, Pennsylvania. The document is in German and is easily translated into English without much or any knowledge of German simply by using a guide to German church records or a dictionary. The name of the mother of the child may be misinterpreted, however, if one concludes that she was Susanna Beitlerin. In German that would be true because the feminine form of a name has the ending "in." Because English has no such gender

68

counterpart for surnames, Susannah's maiden name would actually be rendered as Beitler and that form of the surname would be the one which her father bore.

Ethnic Clues

The prefixes "Mc," "Mac," and "M'" are Gaelic for "son of." All three are found in both Scotland and Ireland. In the seventeenth century it was the English practice to index the surname by the stem of the name rather than by the patronymic Mc, Mac, or M' so John McGill would appear in the G section of the alphabet. A few families are distinctively found in only one of the British Isles and that situation can certainly narrow the scope of genealogical research.

Examples of such are:

Irish	Scottish
McBride	McKay
McCall	McClintock
McCreary	McCloud
McDaniels	McSwain
McElroy	McClung
McGill	

Other surnames from the Mc category may have different spellings in each country. McLain is the Irish spelling, and McLean is the Scottish family.

In the borders. the West Highlands, and fishing villages of Scotland, the number of distinctive surnames in communities might be no more than four or five. The village of Findochty in Banffshire had 182 families but only four surnames:, viz. Flett, Sutherland, Smith, and Campbell. Different forenames were also not plentiful so the inhabitants adopted a "to-name" or nickname which followed the surname in order to establish their identities. The to-name might have been the name of a wife, name of a parent, or the name of a fishing boat.

The Name Is the Game: Onomatology and the Genealogist

If a Scottish surname is identified as being " Egyptian," it designates a Gypsy.

"O'" in Ireland is for "grandson of" as in O'Donnell. Prefixes are also subject to exceptions. Someone named Osteen is not an Irishman who ceased to use the apostrophe but instead of an English family named Austin.

Sometimes a surname has become so conspicuous in America that a genealogical presumption would seem to be the only explanation possible. While Jose might appear to be an Hispanic surname, it was in fact a colonial family in Maine established by Christopher Jose who arrived at the Isle of Shoals in 1651. The surname of Luna might be perceived as the Spanish version of the surname of Moon in English. It can also, however, be a modified spelling of the Manx surname of Looney from the Isle of Mann.

The suffix "-ski" is found in both Germany and Poland. The suffix was indicative of one who owned land. The higher incidence in America of "-ski" among Poles might seem to indicate that Poles appropriated the suffix and climbed up the social ladder by adding it to their surnames. The suffix "-sen" is used by the Danes, but the suffix "-sson" is Swedish. Norwegians use both "-sen" and "-son."

"Fitz" is a Norman French prefix meaning "son of." It is no longer found in France but is found in the British Isles. Fitzgerald and Fitzmaurice are usually Irish."Van" meaning "of" is a prefix for a Dutch surname as in Van Zandt. It is, however, also found in Germany as in Ludwig Van Beethoven. Another Dutch prefix is "Ten" as in William Ten Broek. "Von" with a lower case "v" occurs in Germany and also means "of." While von may be an indication of German nobiliary status, it would be written as the abbreviation "v." rather than spelled out in full in the church books. If the preposition is spelled out in full in a church book, the entry pertains to a commoner.

"Ap" is the Welsh word for "son of." Its feminine counterpart is

The Name Is the Game: Onomatology and the Genealogist

"verch." The patronym tended to become fused to the forename of the father so that John ap Rhys became John Price, John ap Howell became John Powell, John ap Owen became John Bowen, John ap Evan became John Bevan, Griffin ap Harry became Griffin Parry, and John ap Richard became John Prichard.

In 1935 Merrow Edgerton Sorley proposed that John Lewis was a scion of the Lewis family of Warner Hall. While the lands of two Lewis families were no more than five miles apart, they were separate and distinct. Later day descendants commissioned the College of Arms to grant arms with out any substantiation. Dr. Malcolm Harris excavated tombstones on the plantation which had been in Lewis family. One stone stated John Lewis was born in Monmouthshire and died 21 August 1657 aged 63 years. The Lewis plantation in Virginia bore the name of Port Holly. In 1957 John Manahan recognized that Port Holly was actually the name of the parish of Llantilio Pertholey in Monmouthshire. A search of the parish register would have been futile unless one knew that Rycketts was a Welsh colloquialism for the possessive case, English language equivalent of Richards. The baptismal entry indicated that John, the son of Lewis Rycketts, was baptized 22 February 1591/92, ap Richard. John Lewis was actually the son of Lewis and the grandson of Richard. His marriage entry on 3 February 1610 identifies him as Johane Lewis Pricket. i.e. John, the son of Lewis, and the grandson of Richard. The will of Richard Lewis dated 15 March 1627, and probated a month later on 18 April 1828, identified two sons, Edward Prichard and Thomas Prichard. Grace McLean Moses unraveled the clues in her work *The Welsh Lineage of John Lewis (1592-1657) Emigrant to Gloucester, Virginia.*

Statutory Changes
One of the more obscure factors genealogists overlook is the change of name by colonial or state statute.

Colonial, territorial, and state governments provided for legal changes of names by the legislature. Gradually each jurisdiction opted to delegate the task to county and district courts. Iowa was one of the earliest states to do so. Delaware was the only one of the thirteen original states still offering legislative name changes in the twentieth century.

Legislative name changes came about for a variety of reasons including the resumption of a maiden name by a divorced woman, legitimations, inheritances, and adoptions. The enmity between the parties in divorce proceedings may have been so strong that the wife not only resumed her maiden name but also had the surname of her children changed to hers as well.

Personal reasons also accounted for name changes. New born babes were often given a diminutive at birth rather than the full form of a forename. Children might be named Polly and Billie rather that Mary and William. When they attained their majority, they were resentful that their forenames were those born by children rather than adults, so they resorted to legislative name changes to overcome the stigma of not having actual forenames.

Maryland was the only jurisdiction where legislative name changes involving inheritances of property, both real and personal, also included the right for a family kinsmen through a female branch to use a coat-or-arms of a maternal grandfather by changing his surname to that of his armigerous forbear. Examples included James Maccubin who became James Carroll and Charles Ridgeley Carnan who became Charles Ridgeley.

Sometimes the name change is due to the fact that the surname is considered to be crude in English. One of the most common change of name in Massachusetts involves the surname Hoar because it so closely resembles "Whore." In New Hampshire more than a hundred individuals with the surname Hogg had their surname legally changed. The same also applied to those bearing the surname Leathers in the Granite Mountain State. Any surname with the suffix of "-cock" such as Woodcock, Haycock,

The Name Is the Game: Onomatology and the Genealogist

Hitchcock, and Glasscock would likely be legally changed to something less suggestive of the male reproductive organ. The Pennsylvania Dutch surname Scheitz is equally embarrassing. By act of the Missouri legislature Peter, Jacob, Joseph, Frank, Margaret, and Christian Hintershit had their surname changed to Hinters 2 March 1853. Bernard John Focking, Mary Ann Focking, and John B. Focking had their surname changed to Bennett by legislative action in Illinois 31 January 1837.

Sometimes the surname is less than pleasant to the bearer leading to a legal change of name as in Wormwood to Wood or Forest.

Some names are simply too unwieldy. Thomas DePrarar DeLeBett Marac Fearegius LeLaedzedar in Maine was changed to Thomas Adams which English-speaking Americans could accommodate in 1832.

Immigrants often shed their identity by taking an English name which aided in acculturation. Pesanti Sanchez of Salem, Massachusetts in 1830 took the name of George Leon. Pedro Blassina of Beverly, Massachusetts became Edward Harrington in 1832, and Petro Papathakes of Boston took the name of Peter Peterson in 1831.

The change of name legislation may also apply to forenames. Susannah Cremer of Greene County, Tennessee, although a male, bore a female forename from birth. His parents dressed him in female attire which he wore to a mature age. In 1827 he had his name changed to William Cremer. He was not the one who inspired Johnny Cash's song, "A Boy Named Sue." That individual was Judge Sue Kerr Hicks of Madisonville, Tennessee, who was the prosecutor in the famous Scopes Trial in 1925. He was named after his mother, Susanna (Coltharp) Hicks, who died giving birth in 1895.

Some changes of name are effected in order for an heir to receive a legacy from a family member who in his or her will made such a conditional bequest. Still other changes of names are effected in order to establish legitimacy so that one's offspring can inherit. On 23 August 1822 by Tennessee statute, James Black, John Black, and Jesse Black of Overton County were authorized to alter their names to James Carmack, John Carmack, and Jesse Carmack in order to make them legitimate and to become eligible to inherit the estate of their father, Jesse Carmack.

The Georgia legislature enacted a change of names to Hudson for James Walton Whitehead, Martha Amanda Whitehead, Sarah Elizabeth Whitehead, Nancy (Whitehead) Honge the wife of Darius Honge, and Sophia (Whitehead) Thompson the wife of Robert Thompson to Hudson. Unfortunately, the topographer who set the type of the published act misread their new surname so the act had to be amended on 23 December 1839 to the corrected surname of Hendon. They were the reputed illegitimate children of James Hendon of Clarke County, Georgia. William Stotesbury of Chatham County, Georgia had his name changed to William Sobieski McFarland on 31 December 1838, but the act did not indicate the reason why he did so.

Adoption can also be the basis for a legal change of name. Augusta Shilling, daughter of Gustav Shilling, deceased, was adopted by Charles and Mary Ann Winters of Lexington, Fayette County, Missouri, and they had her name changed to Augusta Winters.

By an act of the legislature of Virginia passed 13 December 1833, Jacqueline P. Howle, Martha C. Howle, Mary C. Howle, and Matilda C. Howle of New Kent County had their surname changed to Poindexter.

By act of 2 March 1837, Overton T. Lowry and his sister, Pamelia Lowry, the children of Aaron and Mary Lowry, of Louisa County, Virginia, had their names changed to Overton T. Gardner and Pamelia M. Gardner.

Foundlings are another basis for a change of name statute. One Thaddeus of St. Charles County, Missouri, had his name changed to Thaddeus Franklin, 17 February 1843. He was an infant when he was found along the roadside in Franklin County, Virginia and eventually took the name of the locality of his nativity as his surname.

Thomas Hanlon of Pennington, Mercer County, New Jersey had a father who had been dead for more than half a century. He and the rest of the children were minors at the time and believed that their father's name was Hanlon and that his middle initial was O. Thomas Hanlon had his surname changed to the corrected form of O'Hanlon by act of the New Jersey legislature 17 March 1898 when he learned the difference and sought to forego any legal difficulties due to the misunderstanding.

Surnames which were too unwieldy to English-speaking America also tended to be changed. Stephen Joseph Iankiewicz had his surname changed by the Illinois General Assembly 3 March 1843, to Stephen Joseph Dallas.

Augustine Demetrius Gallitzen of Pennsylvania assumed the alias of Smith. Later in life he wished to resume his former surname and did so by statute.

District and County Court Changes of Names
Iowa was one of the first states in the nation to place the responsibility of a legal change of name with the district courts thereby relieving the state legislature from the task. In Webster County, Iowa, in March 1884, three brothers, Ole E. Haatvedt, Nils E. Haatvedt, and Thor E. Haatvedt, had their names changed to Ole E. Edwards, Nils E. Edwards, and Thor E. Edwards. The decree indicated that they were born 21 Nov. 1838, 12 Mar. 1834, and 6 Oct. 1843 respectively. In addition to their height, hair color, and eye color, their place of nativity was reported as Norway, and their parents were Evan Aslakson and Ingobor Oleson.

Multiple Independent Appearances
It should also be noted that the same surname may be introduced in more than one country. Brody or Brodie, for example, is found not only in

Ireland and Scotland but also in Russia and Germany. Martin is probably the most widespread surname found in many European languages. A surname without genealogical details cannot be attributed to its ethnicity.

Alexander Balmain was a Presbyterian minister in Frederick County, Virginia, who performed the marriage of Joshua Potts and Milly Suvilly on 3 August 1797. He recorded the bride under her diminutive for Amelia. Her grand-daughter recorded that her grandmother's maiden name was Milly Souber. Certainly the letters "b" and "v" may be interchangeable as are "l" and "r", but it is unclear if this is the explanation for the discrepancy.

Consider the Slafter family of New England. Descendants use not only that spelling but also Slaughter and Slater. In Virginia Robert Slaughter also appeared as Robert Slater in Old Rappahannock County. Both families were of English stock. The spelling of Slaughter has also been adopted by descendants of Pennsylvania Dutch Schlatters and New Netherland Dutch Sluyters.

Spanish

In many Spanish speaking countries the surname of the father and of the mother are reflected in the surname of their offspring. If Pedro Perez Montilla married Leocadia Blanco Alvarez, their son, Antonio could appear in one of four ways. He could be Antonio Perez Blanco [his father's and his mother's surnames], as Antonio Perez-Blanco [the hyphenated union of his father's and his mother's surnames], as Antonio Perez y Blanco [the symbol for reflecting his father's and his mother's surnames], or as Antonio Perez Montilla y Blanco Alvarez [his father's paternal and maternal surnames and his mother's paternal and maternal surnames]. The two most common patterns reflecting the paternal and maternal heritage is the joining of the two by the character "y" or the hyphen.

This practice is especially useful because of the high percentage of individuals bearing the surnames of Garcia, Martinez, Fernandez, Lopez,

The Name Is the Game: Onomatology and the Genealogist

Gonzalez, and Rodriguez.

African-American

Like other non-Europeans African-Americans adopted surnames. Since
Europeans created the religious, court, and business records, they reflected
the cultural pattern of recording others without surnames. The absence of
surnames in the records themselves, however, does not mean that African-
Americans lacked surnames.

In the evacuation of the British and Loyalists from New York City in
1783, there were more than 3,000 blacks and mulattos nearly all of whom
appeared with surnames. The records also reveal the names of their most
recent owners, and their surnames were not the same as their former owners.
In the century and a half preceding the Civil War and the general
emancipation, most slaves had different surnames than their owners. Many
of those who were born in West Africa were baptized Roman Catholic
Christians due to the efforts of the Portuguese. These surnames were those
of remoter ancestors.

Male African-American given names include Juba, Mimbo, Mango,
Mingo, Quash, Wquaco, Quoma, and Vigo. Female African forenames
include Cutto, Tenah, and Cudja. Mima could also have an African origin,
but it could also be the diminutive of Jemima, one of Job's daughters. Many
black African-Americans bore the forename of Scipio, a leader of the Roman
Empire who saw military service in north Africa. Other classical forenames
were Cato, Pompey, and Caesar. Such classical names were usually given to
house servants rather than field hands during slavery.

The surnames of Cumbo, Cuffy, and Chavis are often indicative of
Black African-Americans.

The term "Ethiopian" was also used to designate anyone of black

77

African descent. It had no geographical specificity on the continent of Africa.

A surname beginning with the letter "Q" may very well be a clue that the bearer is a Black African American as in the example of Revolutionary War pensioner, Cato Quasha, of Tolland County, Connecticut.

Legal changes of names for African-Americans established that free men of color were entitled to a surname. Examples include David Tuppence in 1826 in Alabama, Richard Webb in 1836 in Maryland, Frank Lytle in 1794, Edward Gauntlett in 1810 in North Carolina, and Richard Webb in 1836 in Rhode Island. Cuffee Potter had his name changed to George Potter in 1838 in Rhode Island.

Jewish

One of the naming practices of Ashkenazi Jews was not to honor an ancestor by bestowing his or her forename on a descendant until the ancestor was deceased; otherwise, the person's soul would be disturbed after death. Sephardic Jews did not observe this practice.

Sephardic Jews would name the eldest son for his grandfather and the eldest daughter for her grandmother whether the grandparent was alive or dead.

Jews were subject to the laws of the nation in Europe in which they resided. In 1781 Emperor Joseph II of Austria issued the Edict of Toleration for Jews. It required Jews to take surnames. (It did not apply to Silesia until four years later.) In 1787 the edict was extended to cover all of the Austrian provinces; Hungary was not included. Jews had to register their choices, and the fee for their choice was graduated so that the most desirable surnames cost the most. Gems and flowers such as Goldstein and Rosenthal were more expensive than Ochseschwanz (ox tail).

The Name Is the Game: Onomatology and the Genealogist

In 1808, Napoleon required all Jews in the empire to take family names. They could not select names of famous families or of localities. The Kingdom of Prussia emancipated Jews in 1812 on the proviso that they adopt family names. The law applied to Posen in 1833 and the rest of the Prussian Empire in 1845.

In 1844 the Russian Empire compelled Jews to register their names. The decree also applied to Poland where Jews had been required to use family names since 1821.

Two kinds of patronymics exist for Jews. The Hebrew, "ben" meaning son, would appear between the given name of the son and his father's given name as in Moses ben Maimonides. Sometimes the "ben" elides with the forename as in Benelisha meaning son of Elisha. The Ashkenazi Jews used a suffix at the end of the name for "son of." The suffix would be governed by the language of the country involved. Abramowitz, Abrahamowski, and Abramson would be for son of Abraham. Hebrew can also use the genitive terminal "s" for the same purpose, as in Abrahams and Abrams.

Jews who left their home community and relocated elsewhere in Europe might become known by their previous place of residence. Navarro, Leon, and Castro are such examples and are often preceded by the preposition "de" meaning "from " as in "de Costa." A Jewish rabbi, Meir Katzennellenbogen (1482-1565), who left Katzenellenbogen, Germany and went to Padua, Italy, adopted as his surname his former place of residence. Among his descendants are Karl Marx, Helena Rubinstein, Martin Buber, and Felix Mendelsohn. Other Jewish surnames derived from former places of residence include Halpern, one who came Heilbrunn; Dreyfus, one who came from Treves (Trier); and Schwab, one who came from Schwabia.

In areas of Europe where Jews were forced to take surnames and pay rather exorbitant fees for somewhat disparaging surnames, the result may alter their original pejorative meaning. The surname of Goldwasser, or urine,

The Name Is the Game: Onomatology and the Genealogist

loses its distasteful origin in the English counterpart of Goldwater.

American Indian Surnames

While most American Indians adopted European surnames due to intermarriage, there are some which are peculiar to American Indians. Mankiller, Bigfeather, Hummingbird, Stayathome, and Walkingstick are Cherokee tribal surnames. Birdsong might seem to be another, but it is oftentimes actually the English translation of the German surname Vogelsanger.

The Name Is the Game: Onomatology and the Genealogist

Chapter 4 Toponyms

Geographical names can also pose difficulties for the genealogist. In the seventeenth century, "Virginia" or the "Virginias" was a term designating all of British mainland North America so records in England referring to a colonist who was in Virginia may be quite misleading. He did not have to have been a resident within the boundaries of modern day Virginia. By the eighteenth century European lack of geographical knowledge of the New World is reflected in references to the Island of Pennsylvania in church books in Germany to indicate the place a villager had gone to the New World in the eighteenth century. Pennsylvania was the only English colony uniting to form the United States of America with no water frontage on the Atlantic Ocean.

A "Barbadian" in colonial South Carolina and elsewhere on the mainland of British North America was a term applied to anyone from one of the English island colonies in the Caribbean, including Grenada, Antigua, Bahamas, Jamaica, Nevis, St. Christopher, as well as Barbados.

A nineteenth-century obituary of someone who died in Texas reported the place of nativity of the decedent as Yellow Bushes County, Mississippi. It was, in fact, Yalabousha County, Mississippi. Sinkler County, Alabama was actually St. Clair County, Alabama. For Americans unfamiliar with European geography, one will encounter the state of birth of a German immigrant as Barren in the census records. He was actually from Bayern, i.e. Bavaria. In the memorials of South Carolina appears "Pittsy Evania" County, Virginia. The scribe was unacquainted with the place name in the Old Dominion and rendered it phonetically instead of the correct spelling of Pittsylvania County. The county of Laurens in South Carolina and Georgia tends to become Lawrence in other parts of the nation where individuals are

The Name Is the Game: Onomatology and the Genealogist

unfamiliar with spelling.

Both North and South Carolina have a county named Beaufort, but the pronunciations are different. In North Carolina it is pronounced Bo fert, and in South Carolina it is Bu fert.

Colonial records in Louisiana contain numerous references to Isle aux Nois. There is no such locality in the lower Mississippi Valley or the state of Louisiana. It was the phonetic French rendering of Illinois in New France.

Spelling may not be in accord with the pronunciation as in the case of St. Francois County, Missouri, which is pronounced as if it were spelled St. Francis County. It is an instance of a French spelling but an English pronunciation.

Houston, Texas is pronounced as Hughston. In Georgia the county of the same name is pronounced as though it were spelled as Whostun, while the street of the same name in New York City is pronounced as if it were spelled Houseton. The town of Boerne, Texas is pronounced as as though it were written Bernie, and the Texas county of Montague is pronounced as though it were spelled Mon Tag.

Death certificates often have the abbreviation "DK" for the place of birth of the decedent. It does not represent Dakota; instead, it is for "Don't Know." The abbreviation "B.C." for the place of birth in a federal census record in late nineteenth century on the northern border of the country might be interpreted to represent British Columbia. It actually was for Bas Canada meaning Lower Canada rather than western Canada. The abbreviation, "FR," for place of nativity for a resident of Tennessee in a nineteenth century census record, may actually represent the lost state of Franklin rather than France. The state of Indiana was initially abbreviated as "Ia." and should not be interpreted to mean Iowa. The creation of Iowa necessitated changing the abbreviation for the Hoosier State to Ind.

Chapter Five

Selected Bibliography of Legal Change of Names

[CT] Kemp, Thomas J. "Changes of Names from the Resolves and Private Acts of the State of Connecticut," *Connecticut Ancestry,* XXXI (1998), 27-41.

[FL] Wolfe, William A. *Names and Abstracts from the Acts of the Legislative Council of the Territory of Florida, 1827-1845.*

[GA] Bockstruck, Lloyd de Witt, "Name Changes in Georgia by Legislative Act, 1802-1854," *Georgia Genealogical Society Journal,* XXXVI (2000), 218-35 and XXXVII (2001), 2-8.

[GA] Coweta County Genealogical Society, *A Decade of Georgia Information, 1851-1861: Abstracts of Genealogical and Historical Interest from Selected Acts of the Georgia General Assembly.*

[GA] Davis, Robert S. *The Georgia Black Book: Morbid, Macabre, & Sometimes Disgusting Records of Genealogical Value,* II, 31-61.

[GA] Rowland, Arthur R. "Name Changes Legally in Ga., 1800-1856," *National Genealogical Society Quarterly,* LV (1967), 177-210.

[IN] Newhard, Malinda. *Name Changes Granted by the Indiana General Assembly to 1852.*

[KY] Nave, Doris. *Kentucky Frontiersmen: Name Changes, Legitimations, and Adoptions Found in the State of Kentucky, 1802-1850.*

[LA] Rieffel, Judy. *Genealogical Selections from the Acts of the Louisiana Legislature, 1804-1879.*

[MD] Meyer, Mary K. *Divorces and Names Changed in Maryland by Act of the Legislature, 1834-1854.*

[ME] King, Marquis F. *Changes in Names by Special Acts of the Legislature of Maine 1820-1895.*

[MA] *List of Persons Whose Names Have Been Changes in Massachusetts*

1780-1892.

[MN] Green, Stina H. *Adoptions and Name Change, Minnesota Territory and State, 1855-1881.*

[MO] Bockstruck, Lloyd de Witt. "Legal Change of Names in Missouri prior to 1868," *Missouri State Genealogical Association Journal,* XXVII (2007), 7-12.

[NH] Index to the Laws of New Hampshire Recorded in the Office of the Secretary of State 1679-1883.

[NH] Roberts, Richard P. *New Hampshire Name Changes, 1768-1947.* 2 vols.

[NJ] *Legal Name Changes 1847-1947.* [Database on line on the web page of

the New Jersey State Archives.]

[NY] Austin, John. "Early Changes of Name in New York," *The New York Genealogical and Biographical Record,* CXXVII (1996), 137-42 & 222-25, CXXXVIII (1997), 44-48 & 97-100.

[NY] Scott, Kenneth. *Petitions for Name Changes in New York City,* 1845-1899.

[NC] McBride, Ransom. "Legal Name Changes by Act of North Carolina Assembly 1790–1808," *North Carolina Genealogical* Journal, I (1975), 68-74 and II (1976), 18-23, 162-167.

[OR] Camden, D. *Adoptions and Name Changes State of Oregon 1876-1919.*

[PA] Livengood, Candy Crocker. *Genealogical Abstracts of the Laws of Pennsylvania & the Statutes at Large.*

[RI] Taylor, Maureen. *Name Changes in Rhode Island 1800-1880.*

[SC] Holcomb, Brent H. "Some Legal Name Changes in South Carolina," *South Carolina Magazine of Ancestral Research,* XIII (1985), 123.

[TN] Miller, Alan. *Nineteenth Century Tennessee Adoptions, Legitimations, and Name Changes.*

[TX] McWilliams, Rena Doughty. *Abstracts of the Laws of Texas 1822-1846.*

[VA] Peppenger, Wesley E. *Connections and Separations: Divorce, Name*

The Name Is the Game: Onomatology and the Genealogist

Changes, and Other Genealogical Tidbits from the Acts of the Virginia General Assembly.

[**VT**] Bartley, Scott A. "Name Changes in Vermont 1778-1900," *Vermont Genealogy,* IX (2004), 1-56.

[**UK**] Phillimore, William. *Index to Changes of Names under Authority of Changes of Names.*